WELCOME ABOARD

INSIDE THE WORLD'S GREAT CLASSIC YACHTS

TEXT AND PHOTOGRAPHY BY

MATTHEW WALKER

FIRST GLANCE BOOKS

Cobb, California

Published by
First Glance Books, Inc.

© 1998 O.G. Publishing Corp.

Distributed by
First Glance Books, Inc.
P.O. Box 960
Cobb, CA 95426
Tel (707) 928-1994
Fax (707) 928-1995

ISBN 1-885440-34-0

Printed in Hong Kong

Produced by
American Graphic Systems, Inc.
P.O. Box 460313
San Francisco, CA 94146
Fax (415) 285-8790

Book and Cover Design by
Crowfoot Design Group
Tel (707) 928-4038

Text and photos © Matthew Walker

Table of Contents

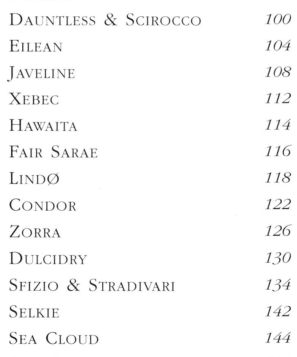

Introduction

Call me irresponsible. A few years ago, having no better prospects ashore, I took a job as a "boatbuilder." It's one of those dirty, unappreciated types of work which the outside world ignores, possibly because boatbuilding offers absolutely no opportunity of social advancement and certainly no chance for wealth and fame. But I was happy, and while most of my fellow wage-earners have to breathe recycled air and stare into computer displays all day long, at least I could enjoy sunlight and the smells of saltwater and cedar shavings. I started to take a lot of photographs of my fellow boatbuilders at work, mostly so that I could convince my relatives and friends that my vocation did, in fact, produce a useful end result.

In my case, I was building "custom" sailboats in the highly-respected Thomas Wylie Design shop in Alameda, California. Most of the sailboats I worked on were nice, respectable family yachts — sleek fiberglass hulls with practical, easy-to-maintain wood interiors and just enough equipment for a comfortable weekend cruise with the kids. On the other hand, a few of our customers chose race-winning sailboats or fully-equipped luxury cruiser/racers. I had the unique opportunity to work on these special projects while carefully recording (in literally thousands of color transparencies) both their construction and the finished products. And I was surprised to discover that good, old-fashioned wood has again become just as popular for high-tech yacht design as have exotic materials, such as carbon fiber, Kevlar®, and space-age composites.

I got rather excited about this modern renaissance in boatbuilding and "classic" yacht design. I even published articles in Sail, Yachting, Wooden Boat, and other magazines, and eventually I wrote a book entitled Down Below, which was well recieved and contained photos I has taken of beautiful, often very famous, sailing yachts and motor yachts from around the world. But in retrospect, I think I missed something. As an eager young author/photographer, I was writing about the subject of boats in the same fragmented way that a committee of blind men, each of them having handled widely-separated parts of a huge elephant, would offer their very different appraisals of the patient pachyderm.

This book is an attempt, not merely to describe the lumps, bumps, and wrinkles of various individual boats and boatowners, but instead to explore inside the fine art of "yachting." Those readers who might want more technical and historical details about vessels in this book or future projects are invited to visit my Worldwide Web site at the Internet address shown below. (The same invitation applies to any reader in the movie business who's keeping a sharp eye out for a salty novel and screenplay!)

During a lifetime spent messing about in boats, I have been lucky enough to meet an amazing crew of wonderfully talented, generous sailors and boatbuilders. Their help and cooperation made this book possible.

Matthew Walker
Alameda, California
Internet — http://www.diosa.com/

High-Tech Traditional

When prehistoric sailors first discovered that they could tie or peg a few logs together to create boats a bit more seaworthy than their original dugout canoes, they also realized that the surrounding water was still capable of leaking through any open seams in their boats. For the past several thousand years, that basic problem has remained the focus of all boatbuilding and shipbuilding — whether in wood, steel, aluminum, fiberglass, concrete, or what-have-you. Simply put, no matter what material you use, it has to "keep the water out."

Until recently, wooden boatbuilding had fallen out of favor, except among hardcore traditionalists and do-it-yourselfers. Even the most precise plank-on-frame wood construction will leak; it requires regular re-caulking, sanding, painting, and so on. (Understandably, most boatbuyers would rather purchase a cheap, low-maintenance plastic boat and spend their limited leisure time on the water, instead of chasing down leaks in their boat bottoms). Among designers of custom or limited-production sailboats and powerboats, the favored hull materials had become fiberglass, aluminum, and often steel — even though these designers would freely admit that wood was "potentially" the best boatbuilding material available.

Then (after World War II) came the development of truly waterproof glues, especially marine-grade epoxy. Two revolutionary changes in wooden yacht design immediately took effect. First, a yacht builder could now laminate an entire wooden hull and its interior components into a single, incredibly stiff, lightweight shell, what racing-car folks call "monocoque" construction. And second, if that hull were completely coated and sealed inside and out with waterproof epoxy, then it would never need caulking of any kind, and it would be nearly immune to all the decay, wood worms, chemical or galvanic corrosion, and other underwater ailments which have plagued wooden boats for thousands of years. Great stuff, this epoxy.

hen I first started work as a boatbuilder, I was assembling and installing plywood interiors into fiberglass sailboats at the Thomas Wylie Design shop. All I knew about epoxy glue was that it was insanely strong, especially when it had glass "microfibers" or "microballoons" mixed in, and also that setting a large cup of activated epoxy out in the sun could produce a hot, smoking corkscrew of toxic, slowly-expanding epoxy foam — what chemists calmly refer to as an "exothermic reaction." Another thing I learned was that different epoxy resins could be be activated and cured using either a separate hardener liquid, or simply an external heat source, or sometimes even microwave radiation. Even so, my only interest in epoxy, especially on warm summer days, was to get all my assembly work done before the damn glue hardened!

The Gemini racers (nicknamed "The Twins") changed all that. Our shop had an order for one of these sexy new wood/epoxy racers, which we would build using the trademarked "WEST System" (wood/epoxy saturation technique), perfected by Gougeon Brothers. The buyer was none other than George Kiskaddon, a very experienced California sailor and founder of the Oceanic Society in San Francisco. Tom Wylie and a few friends decided to finance an identical sailboat, so the new baby became "twins." The two boats started to take shape, as a bunch of formerly all-fiberglass builders found themselves laminating multiple layers of thin cedar veneers over a

plastic-sheathed, upside-down, temporary wooden mold — and visitors from all along the waterfront stopped by to peek curiously at our strange work.

This was not your average boatbuilding. Most traditional wooden sailboats have rows of thick ribs, and a backbone, and all sorts of internal transverse bulkheads and beams that provide strength and offer some reassuring resemblance to the inside of a house, or at least a barn. But, after being lifted off the mold, The Twins looked like completely empty eggshells, with the boldly-striped cedar veneers showing through the clear epoxy and transparent fiberglass cloth. As work progressed, only a few interior components were added: some wooden "ring frames," laminated in place to stiffen the hull; a plywood engine box (with tiny, gimballed camping stove); two tiny benches; and a manual bilge pump. These were extreme, radical, ultralight, stripped-out racing boats, with not one compromise for any handicapping rule or measurement system.

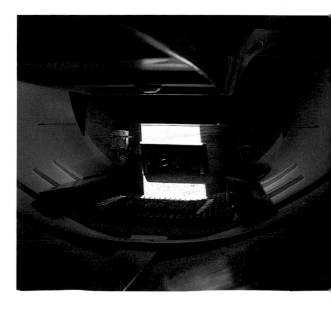

A conventional person will divide the world into Business, Arts, Science, Sports, and similar cut-and-dried categories. Boatbuilders are rarely conventional. I would argue that their unforgiving line of work requires far better engineering and design skills than, say, house carpentry and residential architecture. After all, how often do you navigate your house through storms and dangerous shallows? A yacht must perform all the same domestic and structural tasks as does a house, but the yacht doesn't have the cozy privilege of sitting still, high, and dry on its foundation while doing so.

Some boatbuilders and yacht designers have acquired not only the necessary engineering skills, but have reached the level where their work must be considered a form of "art." A master watchmaker's tiny jewelled timepiece, a carpet-weaver's woolen landscape, a flawless varnished row-boat built in a backyard shed — I'm the sort of person who considers these achievements at least equal to any dusty painting in some local museum.

So when it comes time to "finish" a boat, a few yacht designers leave their artistic signature with a great flourish on the interior or exterior of their creation. Nearly every custom yacht gets the usual bronze plaque naming its designer and builder, but only a few special (and admittedly more expensive) vessels get "the full treatment."

In the case of The Wylie Twins, the designer and owners decided in favor of a transparent epoxy and fiberglass cloth for the boats' protective exterior sheath. On top of that went a super-hard, sunlight-defying, linear-polyurethane varnish. Not cheap. Very spectacular. It amplifies the natural grain and colors of Bruynzeel® mahogany plywood and western red cedar veneers. People reach out carefully toward these boats' glistening sides, trying to fathom that invisible surface.

The only reason that I, a casual weekend sailor and relatively inexperienced woodworker, ever got a job in the Thomas Wylie Design boatshop was that I just happened to walk in on the very day when a new Wylie client paid his first invoice. A big invoice. In other words, the Wylie shop urgently needed to train some new recruits to handle the new business, and I suddenly became a junior assistant apprentice boatbuilder. I would have to learn fast in this place, because the pace

of their construction activity was about to increase dramatically.

The new boat was to be called NO GO 8, and the new client was Elliot Siegel from Chicago, Illinois. He wanted an all-out lightweight racing sailboat, built with the very latest technology and hardware and electronics and sail fabrics and so on, but he also wanted a beautiful and lavishly-appointed luxury cruiser. The latter requirement normally translates as "heavy" in the language of yacht design. After the client

and the designer had hammered out a rea-
sonable balance between these extremes, the
result was a 42-foot, high-performance sloop
to be built with a wood/epoxy lamination
system similar to The Twins' design. The main
difference was that NO GO 8's much thicker
hull would not be laminated over and then
removed from a temporary strip-planked
mold. Instead, the strip plank would become
a permanent part of NO GO 8's hull.

So, as I quickly learned to build yacht
interiors and then to help wet-sand and pol-

ish the nearly-complete Twins, we also
started construction on NO GO 8. The first
steps were to laminate ring-frames of thin
mahogany plank with thickened epoxy,
using a wall-mounted bending jig and
dozens of screw clamps. Nasty, sticky
work, especially on a hot day indoors in
California. The frames, once the glue had
cured, were precisely tapered with electric
planes so that maximum frame thickness
would be down where the boat's lead keel
threatens to flex the hull bottom.

Building a traditional wooden boat hull can be done entirely "by eye," and the result can be quite seaworthy, beautiful, and significantly unsymmetrical. For example, Venetian gondolas are intentionally built so that they tilt dramatically until their human crew and passengers take their proper positions. However, for a modern racing sailboat which must get measured and "rated" under all sorts of mathematical race-handicap formulae, a lopsided hull is simply out of the question. Also, it takes very little distortion in a boat's shape to produce an embarassing incline either to port or to starboard, or even fore and aft. Some minor tilts of this kind are prevented by surreptitiously "pre-launching" a boat a few nights before its first public launch, and if the boat floats with, for example, its nose

down and hindquarters up, then the designer or builders can quickly move a little lead ballast around to achieve correct trim. This emergency practice is rarely discussed with the client, depends obviously on the traditional use of inside movable ballast, and in any event won't work when the boat is seriously heeled over one way or the other.

It's best to avoid all of this in the first place, by measuring, weighing, and assembling the hull materials and interior components with extreme precision. To do this, the seemingly humble "strongback" is often used. Normally just a rigid ladder of massive, wooden beams and heavy bolts, the strongback is usually made perfectly level and must not shift or bend even one centimeter as it begins to support the new boat hull.

NO GO 8 began life as a thin, steel wire, pulled piano-tight high over a heavy strongback on a concrete floor. From that steel wire dangled a "plumb bob," that heavy brass teardrop which slides along under the wire, pointing to the future boat's centerline along the strongback below. The boat's internal bulkheads, ring-frames, and deck beams were supported and locked into place at exactly the correct locations and height over the strongback. After all the frames and large, interior panels were aligned, a full-length, laminated, mahogany "keelson" was glued and bolted along the centerline, locking together all the transverse components.

Once the frames, deck beams, and keelson were assembled for NO GO 8, then the delicate task of "fairing" began. Some frames had to be trimmed slightly around the outer edges or built up with additional laminations. Then the most eagle-eyed and experienced members of the boatshop crew bent extremely long, flexible wood battens over the frames, trying to visualize where the boat hull's inner surface would eventually appear. One builder called this the "voodoo" process, requiring both a reverential attitude and extremely strong black coffee. Other participants in this process ate and drank nothing, certainly not stimulants, and their technique was simply not to breathe at all for several hours.

When fairing has succeeded, then a thousand pencil chicken-scratches and tiny numbers written along the frame edges have recorded exactly how much wood needs to be beveled — shaved off at a precise angle — to align perfectly with the future hull interior. Fairing actually defines where the curved hull lamination will appear in three-dimensional space, and unsightly mistakes can add or subtract buoyancy (a Very Bad Thing). In a few areas, such as along the sides of the

keelson where it meets each frame, additional wood strips are laminated to build up and complete the frames' outer edges. In NO GO 8, as in most other racing boats, nearly all major interior components are firmly bonded to the inside hull surface, creating a rigid, interconnected system of boxes, similar to the interior of airplane wings.

The next step was simply to cover the entire, perfectly fair row of frames with a seamless panel of glued strip plank. The only secret here is that each strip of wood has one round and one hollow edge to grip the next strip glued and stapled against it (just like hardwood floor planks in your house). This is relatively straightforward "grunt work," and we grunted 'round the clock to get the entire hull planked quickly. When complete, the Port Orford cedar strip-plank layer in NO GO 8 provided most of the hull's longitudinal stiffness.

The finished planking was very lightly planed, just enough to remove imperfections from the smooth surface. Next would come "gorilla warfare" — cutting, gluing, and stapling multiple layers of cedar veneer against the hull, often with loud, dangerous electric routers to trim veneer edges.

Stacks of wide cedar veneers were placed on the floor near the strongback. Then several pneumatic staplers with their long air hoses appeared. Automatic glue dispenser/mixers were set up, along with various solvents, boxes of disposable rubber gloves, and tubs of protective skin cream. Dust-masks were issued to each builder, each of whom wore their least favorite old jeans and thrift-store shirts, or equally disposable paper body-suits. (The solvents, which can remove uncured, or even cured, epoxy glue, can as easily dissolve clothes or human skin). A war zone. Eye-goggles were required equipment, to guard against the inevitable flying splinters and staple fragments.

Each wide, cedar veneer, after being glued and stapled in place, left an uneven gap that tapered at both ends. (Imagine the lines of longitude on a world globe). One fast, efficient way to eliminate these gaps is simply to slide an electric router along one veneer edge, cutting a consistently parallel groove through the next veneer — a process called "spiling." The excess veneer edge is cleaned away, and a narrow veneer strip of the same width as the gap is then glued and stapled in place.

The idea is to prevent any and all air-pocket "voids," or lumps in the final laminate, and to ensure that each layer of veneer has a perfect, unbroken epoxy seal. The alternating diagonal layers distribute the wood's grain direction and strength evenly. The final layer of veneers, an unbroken sequence cut from the same original log, was carefully selected for strength and appearance, and the entire hull was sheathed with transparent epoxy and thin fiberglass cloth, and then wet-sanded until perfectly smooth.

Enough physics and technology? What follows is the traditional ceremony known as "rolling her over." (Male boatbuilders long ago may have coined this phrase). Nothing so unnerves a yacht designer as much as having tons of expensive hull materials and many weeks of careful craftsmanship lifted and spun slowly in the air. Apart from the financial risk involved, there's the possibility of human injury and death, and worse still is the chance that a perfectly smooth hull may get scratched. Don't think about it. Go home and sleep while we take care of this. Come back when the roll cage has been rotated 180 degrees on its floor bearings and the hull is safely supported right-side-up from the rafters above. Don't worry, we'll call you if anyone gets killed.

J ust as the boat's ring-frames are faired before hull lamination begins, so must the deck beams be faired before multiple layers of deck plywood are glued, screwed, and nailed down to complete the structural shell. NO GO 8 had a large forward deck-hatch (for sail-handling during races) and a very low raised deckhouse; all these curved panels and edges must be aligned correctly. The long, continuous, laminated spruce "sheer-clamp" along each side of the hull is where the deck lamination must intersect and bond perfectly with the curved edge of the hull.

With hulls assembled upside-down, it's always a relief when the yacht finally gets flipped over. Experienced builders have no problem working indefinitely in an inverted environment, but the younger crew are sometimes seen hanging their heads upside-down very quickly (in case anyone's watching), just to confirm that the starboard thingamajig is, in fact, getting installed on the starboard side. But the real concern is to get the interior as close as possible to completion before it's time to laminate the deck; it's easy to jump in and out of the open hull, but using a proper

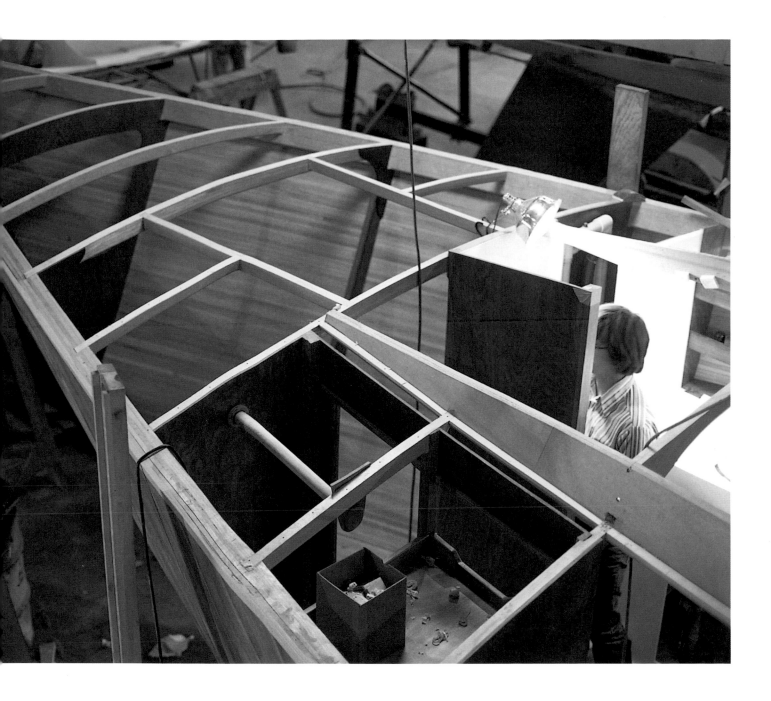

companionway staircase is just too slow (and undignified). And there's the theoretical possibility that someone will forget to install an interior component that won't fit through the deck hatch or companionway....

Any sensible person would agree that it's impossible to combine major, messy structural work (like, say, installing a yacht engine and all fuel supply lines and wiring) with the fine art of varnishing (which requires a dust-free atmosphere and time for each of several coats of varnish to dry completely). But that's what almost happens in a professional boatbuilding shop: Conflicting jobs and schedules must get overlapped in the interest of finishing the job on time. In NO GO 8, final interior assembly was done during the day. Then as much interior varnish as possible was applied early in the evening and allowed to dry overnight. A vacuum cleaner, floodlights and heat lamps, masking tape, top-quality brushes, and deep religious faith are all that's needed to prepare a good coat of varnish — along with a really big stereo to play your favorite music.

When visitors watched NO GO 8's plywood deck being laminated, a frequent question was "Why use epoxy glue if those nails and screws hold down the deck?" Actually, the final deck lamination depends almost not at all on metal fasteners; they merely hold down the plywood so that the super-strong, thickened epoxy can seep into all crevices and create an unbroken bond between all wood surfaces.

Another subtle point is that the entire first layer of plywood has been pre-fitted and temporarily screwed in place, so that its contact with the deck beams can be checked and all surfaces to be painted can be marked.

Then all of the first plywood panels are removed, their bonding surfaces on the underside are covered with masking tape, and the surfaces to be painted get sprayed all at once with white, highly-reflectivmarine enamel. When the paint dries and is partially cured, the masking tape is removed and the plywood can be bonded permanently to the deck beams and sheer-clamp.

As the new deck starts to seal the boat, the Big Cleanup becomes part of everyone's life. Every new construction task is completed, but is immediately followed by a careful vacuuming of one's dust and debris. Slowly, a finished yacht interior starts to take shape. In the forepeak, a stainless steel tube framework gets installed; it will secure sailbags, support folding bunks, and provide a skinny ladder for some agile crewmember during future races. The electrician starts to snake multicolored marine-grade wiring underneath and around everyone as they work.

In most luxury yachts, a considerable effort and expense goes into adding a lovely wood or fabric interior within a very ugly fiberglass or metal structure. However, in a wooden yacht such as NO GO 8, most of the actual hull and deck structure can simply be sanded (and sanded and sanded) and then varnished, becoming a beautiful, exposed portion of the final interior. NO GO 8's laminated spruce deck beams are immediate favorites with sailors and landlubbers alike; here's these shiny, sinuous ribbons of layered wood overhead where you can reach right up and rub them. And the solid wood block through which the mast comes plummeting down through the hull keeps the deck from flexing when the mast gets tuned for serious racing.

A few hardcore engineering items are completely visible as well: Bolted to thick, wood bulkheads are metal chainplates that pierce the deck above and connect to the

mast stays. Reinforcing plates and six bolts under each deck-winch are simply left exposed, as are the black, flat metal bars and bolts which reinforce those places where sails attach to the deck. In the aft cabin, a deck-winch's massive coupling joint above a bunk reminds the visitor that this is a serious racing boat. Deck prisms are strategically located so that a tall crewmember's head can't hit them, but they still illuminate the interior. All interior metal fittings are chromed bronze, stainless

steel, or anodized marine aluminum alloy. Gradually all the important structural, mechanical, and electrical items get installed, and only the incidentals like cup holders and paper towel racks need attention. Lots of varnish touch-ups are necessary whenever toolboxes and new equipment get dragged around on a tight schedule, but eventually the interior feels habitable, and all the builders take turns fantasizing about where they'd sail to if NO GO 8 were their floating home.

As soon as the yacht's overhead lights work and water can squirt out of the faucets and shower nozzle (and have somewhere to drain safely), the hardcore electronics get hooked up and tested. Someone sends a message to their wife via satellite, and someone else sends a fax to a local pizza parlor. (The order was three monster-size pizzas with everything except pineapple and anchovies). Testing some of the electronics, such as radar and sonar, must wait until the yacht's launching and builder's trials on San Francisco Bay.

As a visitor explores the nearly complete NO GO 8 interior, she sits at the navigator's table in the aft cabin and notices that a large, hinged portlight can open directly over the chart table. That portlight is mounted high on the front of the cockpit, and while under sail allows direct conversation between the navigator and the helm. A tiny spotlight and a permanent deck prism mounted under the cockpit structure illuminate the navigator's table.

In the "head," or bathroom (luckily, toilets are almost never found in the forward overhangs of a sailing vessel anymore), a shower

yacht interiors is that everything gets varnished, or epoxy-sealed, or oiled, or whatever does the job. That often means completely assembling and then disassembling a major substructure, such as bathroom cabinetry, before it gets painted or varnished, so that all hidden surfaces, screw-holes, end-grain, corner joints, and seemingly unimportant crevices get completely waterproofed. Then the substructure gets assembled and painted again.

The ideal (sometimes attained) is to have the interior of the boat just as impermeable to water as is the deck and hull exterior. Wooden yacht interiors which get built this way often cost more, will last much longer, and will look and smell cleaner during their working life. Such interiors will probably even come up relatively unscathed if the yacht ever fills with water and is salvaged soon without hull damage. Hopefully the same will be true of the yacht owners!

nozzle is mounted where it can spray the entire enclosure; there is no subdivided shower stall, since the head compartment is completely sealed and waterproof, with its own drainage system. A deck prism or a discreetly mounted miniature fluorescent fixture provides just enough light to find that missing bar of soap.

Invisible among all the details of a well-made wooden yacht is the attention paid to completely waterproofing both exposed wood surfaces and hidden joints. One of the secrets I learned while building top-quality

between rollers and heavy object. Don't let the rolling stone block, or perhaps your custom racing yacht, fall over and crush you. Celebrate successful transport of heavy object with strong beer and loud music.

One of the many disconcerting contrasts in a boatbuilding project of this kind is between the sweaty, dangerous "heavy lifting" and the sweet, delicate touches — like giving the boat her name. Right in the middle of all sorts of noise and grinding and hoisting of huge objects, in walks the local master boat-name calligrapher, Al ("Rembrandt") Gerundo, and he suddenly becomes the center of attention. We hurriedly set up a solid, raised platform on which the painter will sit while performing his magic.

Soon a bunch of fascinated boatbuilding veterans and trainees are gathered around, watching the painter as he marks the design, applies slow-drying lacquer, waves a heat lamp over it for just the right number of seconds, and then applies incredibly thin "gold leaf" to the lacquer. A special soft brush pushes the gold leaf gently and uniformly against the sticky letters below. In a few more minutes, the excess gold is rubbed away, falling like immense, sparkling, yellow snowflakes onto the gray concrete below. A few unwitting bystanders, not realizing that each piece of gold leaf is so thin that its value is negligible, dive after the falling flakes and offer them up to the amused painter. He looks down and says, "That's okay. You keep them."

E ventually, NO GO 8's deep fin keel arrived, got several coats of ultra-slick racing bottom paint applied to it, and was locked into the vertical position in a massive steel transport cradle just outside our boatshop. Which meant, of course, that we had to persuade NO GO 8 to leave the safety of the shop, fly through the air, and perch safely — without even the tiniest dent — on top of the keel and thick bronze bolts waiting outdoors.

Boatbuilders don't like to build elaborate, temporary support structures or vehicles for their projects, for the obvious reason that it wastes money — assuming that those structures won't get re-used. So NO GO 8, despite the yacht's glitzy price tag (don't ask), was rolled out of the shop in the same low-tech manner that ancient Egyptians used to roll stone blocks for the Pharaoh's pyramids. Take a few dozen short cylinders made of hard material (we used thick metal pipe sections) and pry up the heavy object, then slip rollers under the entire length of the heavy object, then pull very hard on ropes until the heavy object moves an inch, and then quit for lunch.

After lunch, emulate the wise Egyptians and hitch an old Jeep instead to the ropes, so that you don't hurt your back. Above all, have a reliable way to stop the heavy object if it starts to roll under its own momentum, and keep your fingers clear of that tiny gap

A huge, hydraulic yacht hoist comes crawling down the road one morning, looking like a tremendous, metallic insect hovering over NO GO 8. The hoist gently lifts the yacht into the air, creeps across the driveway, and lowers the yacht ever so lowly onto the keel and cradle outside our shop. A considerable sigh of relief, and work resumes. First and foremost, the skeg and rudder are completed and tested for smooth operation with the steering gear. Approximately 9,384,421 deck fittings (give or take) must be precisely positioned, installed, and checked by the designer. But everyone stands back and keeps quiet when the waterline and bootstripe get painted.

This is the tightrope, the death-defying final high-wire act of yachtbuilding. Purely cosmetic, but nothing is more noticeable than an unsightly squiggle in a boat's colorful bootstripe. So imagine that it is your job to take an ordinary roll of masking tape and apply it to the side of a 42-foot curvaceous boat hull, while you are standing on a raised walkway and below you a certain amount of distracting automobile and pedestrian traffic hums along.

When you have finished your job, a perfect arc of masking tape will have been applied from one end of the yacht to the other. You will have intersected all the nearly invisible pencil-marks which permanently record the vessel's intended waterline under the hull's transparent epoxy/glass sheath. Then you go around to the other side of the boat and do it all over again. Finally, you can go home early and collapse while the painters apply a colorful racing bottom-paint which repels seaweed, barnacles, and any

law of physics which affects hydrodynamic friction.

What's left now is to enjoy (and pay for) the finished yacht. A remarkable amount of champagne gets consumed on Launching Day, and maybe it's the boatbuilders' way of commiserating with and consoling their superb creation when it gets lowered abruptly into The Drink. Soon the mast, rig, and sails have been tuned, and we take NO GO 8 out for builder's trials under the Golden Gate Bridge — where thousands of tourists look down and wonder who's aboard our tiny speck of a sailboat on the deep blue Pacific.

The Classic Yacht Association

Sausalito and Tiburon, and other nearby parts of Marin County, California, radiate a sort of sun-drenched, fog-hatted, idyllic happiness. It's a relatively wealthy area just north of San Francisco, and the local waterfront caters to hundreds of permanent residents and visiting tourists searching for a little bite to eat, or a little gift to take back home, or maybe even a little romance — in whatever form you might require. But nothing is more romantic than overlooking San Francisco Bay from the outdoor deck of a local restaurant, perhaps while sipping some wine with a friend, when lo and behold! — out of the golden mist appears a little parade of classic, traditional power yachts. None of them appears to be in any hurry to go anywhere fast, and in fact they are most likely watching the folks on the waterfront watching them! All of these boats are filled with happy families, most of them dressed in antique period costumes or at least bizarre hats. Musical instruments are common, and colorful flags and banners are flown at every opportunity.

One of the local organizations which hosts such waterborne parades (on any available holiday, or maybe just to honor some obscure celestial event) is called the Classic Yacht Association. Ann Sutter, owner of the diminutive but very historic CHEROKEE, sometimes invites me to participate and take snapshots of the proceedings. It's tempting here to write all sorts of details down about the names, builders, and authentic history of these vessels, but I'll save that stuff for my Internet site. Here I will instead relate what

I've learned about the creation and long-term care of classic yacht associations in general. Most of all, you need a "hostess," or at least a "host" (those sailors like myself who worship an ancient, pagan sea goddess will prefer a hostess, especially if she owns her own yacht). Hosting is not a nautical or technical term. It merely signifies that, while some older gentlemen with expansive voices and silver hair may serve as "commodores" or whatever of your classic yacht association, the cherished role of hostess is reserved for that person who can persuade the weather gods to cooperate, and the participating children not to fall off their assigned yachts, and the older members of the association not to forget on which day they should be ready for the next parade. Furthermore, a host is capable of preventing collisions, political disagreement, marital transgressions, and even ill will when, for example, black-soled shoes leave nasty marks on somebody's carefully scrubbed teak deck. Think of the host as a religious person, one who calms the waters at sea and in the human soul. A really lucky, well-managed classic yacht association will even have more than one host or hostess. Age helps. Wealth is not necessary and may even cause problems. But a kindly disposition and a willingness to teach the civilized art of traditional yachting are absolutely required.

HERMANA is a big, heavy, elegant, old motoryacht. She has a unique history, and certainly has had a series of unique owners, but in one respect this vessel is like most others in the Classic Yacht Association. When the time came to repair or replace some soggy piece of wood or corroded metal aboard this boat, on that day the owner or crew went to the trouble of finding out exactly how the original boatbuilders might have done the job. Then they spent the time and money to do it right, and they have never touched the damn thing again, thank you very much.

That sort of attitude can lead to a few misunderstandings with boatyard personnel. (Choose your boatyard carefully, dearest future owners of traditional yachts!) So, knowing that a job done right often means doing it yourself, many new classic yacht owners quickly transform themselves into fairly proficient woodworkers, or spar-builders, or even engine mechanics.

Aboard HERMANA, the pilothouse contains a mix of original and replacement woodwork. But the general feeling of big, substantial, well-rounded hunks of beautiful wood has been maintained. It's tempting to assume that this is

interior decorating with a masculine touch, but in fact any large sailing or powered vessel which is intended to be truly seaworthy, and which transports crew and passengers in safety while under way, must have an interior which is both strong and comfortable despite constant motion. Bumping into HERMANA's big, rounded edges won't leave bruises on your arms and hips, nor will that pilothouse start to open up and leak when the yacht is pounding through heavy weather.

On the aft deck, HERMANA carries an absolutely gorgeous, yet removable, folding table, easily unbolted from the deck. It matches, in general appearance, the softly curved benches and cushions, and yet it radiates strength.

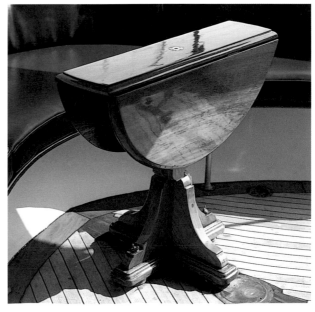

Every classic motoryacht should carry its own ragtime & Dixieland brass band, or so one might think from the way PAT PENDING carries herself during Classic Yacht Association parades and gatherings. This vessel's owner, a San Francisco patent lawyer, makes every effort to have his crew and passengers dress and honk appropriately for every occasion. The only hazard is the unpredictable, cold, and windy San Francisco fog, which can make a big brass tuba or trombone "too cold to kiss."

And flag etiquette is important. Not the burgees and pennants about which old-timers made a remarkable big fuss, but the exact translation of all those letter-and-numeral signal flags hanging overhead. I once met a motor yacht owner in Rhode Island who persisted in using a string of signal flags to spell his mistress' full name, which was quite alright until his wife got suspicious and consulted a marine dictionary he kept aboard. You'll have to decipher PAT PENDING's message for yourself.

PAT PENDING, like many other classic motoryachts, was designed to allow either for completely glass-enclosed comfort in any weather or for leisurely sun-worshipping in several uncluttered locations on deck. The intent was to bring along as many of the interior comforts of home as possible (especially fine dining), while allowing access to the upper decks whenever warm, dry weather permitted.

A quick look at navigation and operating equipment aboard PAT PENDING reminds the visitor that the respectful owner of a large, classic yacht keeps all the original machinery in working order, while prudently supplementing it with very modern electronics. One crew member said it very well: "I'd rather not be the one who insisted on using only historic navigation aids and then got this priceless family yacht ambushed by some uncharted submerged ledge. I run the depth-sounder when the shore gets close."

Amid all the old-time costumes and party atmosphere which PAT PENDING shares with the rest of the Classic Yacht Association, there's a lot of serious, careful seamanship that's preached as well practiced. These are heavy, powerful motor yachts, and they can easily plow right through any lightweight, modern plastic thing that darts accidentally in their way. For example,

it's considered bad form for an Association vessel to hit, or even scrape, a visited dock, because of the resulting stain upon the club's salty reputation, but also because many floating docks nowadays are as easily crushed as the average egg carton.

So it's a pleasure to see Dad, Mom, all the kids, and a few neighbors invited along (not realizing they'd serve as unpaid crew)

for the day's cruise. The boathandling is the first thing. Then comes "learning the ropes," weighing anchor, keeping a watch for watery hazards, setting up lunch on deck, and so on. It's a totally different way of spending your weekend or vacation, and the real beneficiaries are often children — while learning teamwork and safety awareness, they are the first to say how much more fun this is than "sitting in a hot car all day."

And the best part could be that beautiful sunset view along the shore from Belvedere to Tiburon, California, when the Classic Yacht Association has tied up after a busy day on San Francisco Bay, and that dapper musical quartet aboard PAT PENDING gently rocks the waterfront with some almost-forgotten melody.

Speaking of music, have you ever sat right next to a nice old accordion playing romantic, old-fashioned tunes in a very, very small auditorium? Something, say, the size of a nice old motoryacht? Aboard MARCY, a visiting bon vivant was playing an authentic "Soprani" accordion, while his partner in crime fondled a piano keyboard and smiled serenely at passersby on the dock. These gentlemen are accomplished captains and wharf rats, yet they know how to relax, and more importantly, how to relax those around them. At a "formal" gathering of the Classic Yacht Association, nothing breaks the ice better than cheerful, bouncy music.

MARCY is a compact, comfortable vessel, large enough to carry plenty of food and water (and more festive beverages, of course), but small enough to keep the fuel bills manageable. Note the dinghy secured, cradled and covered under the handy boom/davit, used for launching and hoisting the little boat when MARCY is anchored away from shore. The yacht ALLURE obviously resembles PAT PENDING and several other vessels in the Classic Yacht Association, but worth note is the different uses made of available deck space, depending on the vessel's size and the owner's style of cruising.

One of the few required procedures after a classic yacht parade, especially one in which human participants wear outlandish period costumes, is the "Come On Up and See Me Sometime" visit. One by one or in groups, the occupants of various vessels strut their stuff and try to entice each other into reciprocal visits. It's also a great way to discuss and compare paint jobs, new crewmembers, equipment upgrades, and especially the always-newsworthy progress of children and grandchildren.

In an age of high technology and high stress, it should be obvious why the members of the Classic Yacht Association choose to "opt out" — to take a different path. But let me flog this subject a little anyway. I once thought that yachting in general, and traditional yachting in particular, was a rich man's game. Over time, I dis-covered that, with no more wealth than the average household, many families who acquire and restore old sailboats and motorboats have simply focused their income on a very specific goal: that intangible called "quality time." While the rest of the world is out buying new cars every year, along with new TV sets and gadgets and the latest audio or video toys, the typical classic yacht owner has invested in something that requires less money in the long run, but far more sweat.

My own family was typical. My father bought a 31-foot Nova Scotia schooner, a cute little wooden yacht that really was too small to sport two masts and "needed some work." But she was a handy miniature replica of the big, deep-water Canadian fishing schooners of long ago, and in any event the schooner's only purpose initially was to haul our family around the Hudson River on weekends. We called her FOGGY, and we loved her.

We also had to spend a huge amount of time fixing her broken ribs, painting, replacing engine parts, painting, learning about tradi-tional rigging, sanding, and also did I mention painting? As a result, we learned a lot of sailing and do-it-yourself skills, and while other folks were driving from gas station to gas station during their vacations, we were instead taking progressively longer voyages in the coastal waters of New York and New England.

Experiencing all this gives you an appreci-ation for boatbuilding and its implied crafts-manship. Even if you aren't the one who actually creates a wooden yacht, nevertheless, by becoming the fourth or 14th owner, you become part of the yacht's life cycle. You get real close and personal with the structure and history of a seemingly inanimate wooden ves-sel, and you start to appreciate what were once merely "details."

Well, enough of that for now. But do ana-lyze that beautiful teak foredeck and bronze cleat. By getting down on your knees to study these things, you learn to wonder how much effort went into their creation, or for that matter, into the design of a good mariner's compass. Look carefully as well at the dining table set aboard PAPOOSE, with its candlesticks, wine glasses, and silver cutlery. The secret is that everything on that dining table could be pur-chased for not much money at a local antique store. The trick is to conceive of that dining table, to imagine what ingredients would make for a nice Sunday brunch with your best friends. And of course, to have spent a few previous week-ends installing lovely forest-green upholstery and varnishing that folding table. It doesn't always take money, but it does take commitment.

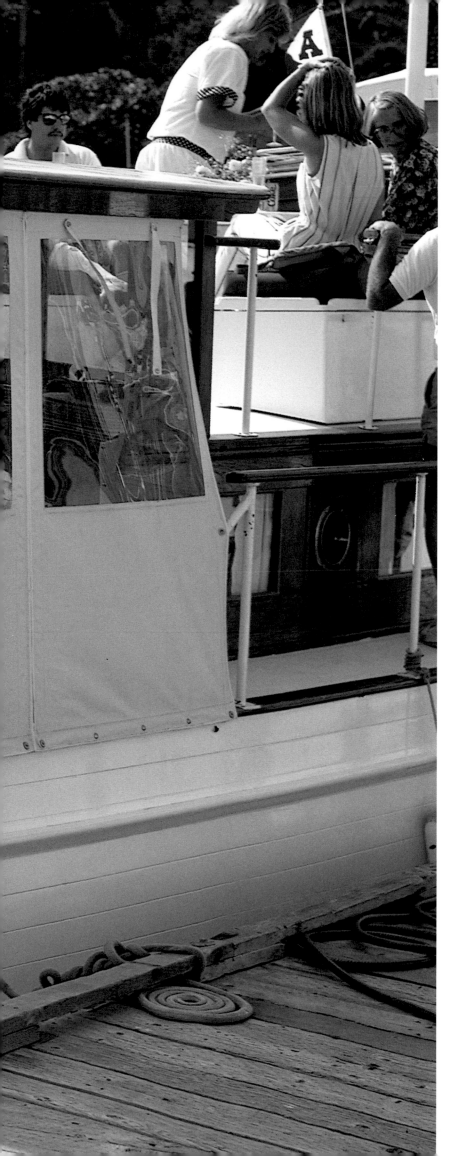

And so, as another parade and gathering of the Classic Yacht Association comes to an end, it's time to kick back and rattle the ice cubes in our glasses. Let us take our places on the aft deck, protected on our shady starboard side by a zippered, transparent roll-up panel, but exposed on the port side to the sun's cheerful rays. We can discuss the day's events, or we can shoot the breeze about anything that crosses our minds. And let us enjoy this final moment when all the yachts, whether they are members of the Association or not, tie up and share a few heartwarming drops from The Auxiliary Fuel Tank.

Along with the big boats, you occasionally find a few charming little classics, like perhaps the antique Chris-Craft runabout QUICK STEP. Here's just the thing for a spin on San Francisco Bay — assuming that you steer clear of the fog, freighters, ferries, and 40-knot winds. QUICK STEP is a gentle reminder that your grandparents' generation knew a few things about Style. They also had the good manners to wear soft-soled "deck shoes" and to raft up their boats two-deep at the dock without a lot of fuss. They had a simple approach to yacht clothing: dressy, and admittedly heavy into whites and blues, but usually not too pretentious. And yet they could be remarkably forgiving of a newcomer's attempts to learn the art of yachting; they had once been new to this game themselves, and they probably even remembered their first invitation to join the parade.

Clearwater

If I were limited to having just one hero, Pete Seeger might be the one. Some people think of him as one of America's finest folksingers and musical historians, and he's also been a forceful, persuasive political activist, upholding the principles of equality and democracy in a selfish, destructive era. But he's probably the one man who should get credit, if not for inventing "the Ecology Movement," then at least for creating its first symbolic success: the Hudson River sloop CLEARWATER.

What all this has to do with "yachting" might seem a little vague, so bear with me. If you, like me, define yachting as the use of any floating vessel primarily for pleasure and recreation, then even a very large traditional replica, such as CLEARWATER, qualifies as a "yacht," for she certainly doesn't turn a profit for her owners. They are a loose organization of volunteers from all walks of life and every profession, sometimes just school-children, who contribute a few dollars for the CLEARWATER cause.

What is that "cause"? In 1969, in a period of American history when police and college students and the urban poor were fighting in the streets of American cities, and when powerful corporations still had the unrestricted ability to poison what came to be known as "the environment," Pete Seeger and a small group of sailors launched a full-size replica of the gaff-rigged wooden sloops which once carried cargo and passengers on the Hudson River. Unlike the original sloops, CLEARWATER's mission would be to promote clean water, clean air, and a healthy respect for our little blue-and-green planet. This was before the world had seen the first photos of Earth as viewed from outer space, and it certainly was before America had even thought seriously about this toxic thing called "pollution."

Soon residents along the heavily polluted Hudson River and in New York City were reading about CLEARWATER's simple message. When it came time to vote on public-works projects or laws to protect the river from radioactive or heavy-metals pollutions, New York residents remembered the cute newspaper pictures and articles about Pete Seeger and CLEARWATER's young, idealistic, fuzzy-headed crew. And those voters enacted some of the strongest, most effective anti-pollution laws that New York had ever seen. Just like that. Which made people elsewhere in America think, and act, and vote for clean air and clean water. This was revolutionary at the time, and nowadays it might seem unlikely that a big wooden sailboat had anything to do with it. But I was there, and that's how it happened.

CLEARWATER has a large, communal sleeping and dining compartment for her volunteer crew. It's rustic, warm, and occasionally filled with spontaneous music and singing. There's a hatch overhead for light and ventilation, and cloth curtains provide something resembling privacy when you sleep. The captain has a tiny, separate cabin, in which you can just barely turn around while putting on a new shirt. The night has been quiet, with only an occasional large ship ghosting by the dock where CLEARWATER rests in preparation for a busy day.

On deck, even though sunrise has yet to lift the fog surrounding Bear Mountain, the ship's carpenter is quietly finishing a few minor repairs, and a cat wanders along before deciding that below deck offers more in the way of warmth, food, and human affection. In the distance, a few cars silently

cross the high suspension bridge linking both sides of the mighty Hudson River.

When the cook prepares a hot breakfast, the aromas are usually enough to wake the sleeping crew. Some volunteers are assigned to kitchen duty, while others climb the steps to the deck and await early-morning instructions from the impatient first mate. Today we are heading upriver to Kingston, New York, there to entertain visiting schoolchildren, their teachers, and their parents while we take aboard a most colorful and unusual cargo: pumpkins. Not merely a few, but hundreds of them, for this is the annual Pumpkin Sail, performed in honor of all the Hudson River sloops long ago, who delivered nearly all of Manhattan's daily consumption of agricultural produce. And Halloween is on the way. . . .

Well, he certainly knows how to please the crowd, hey? Pete Seeger plays a mean banjo, in case you didn't know. (It's inscribed with the motto "This machine surrounds hate and forces it to surrender.") Sometimes the CLEARWATER crew includes a few extra musicians who are able to keep up with one of the giants of American folksinging, and sometimes Seeger just up and sings by himself, counting on dozens of bouncing children to sing along and shake their tail-feathers. These are the young future voters of America you see here, and their just-for-fun antics on the Kingston waterfront will one day translate into a very possessive feeling about their deep, historic Hudson River — one of the longest and most biologically important marine estuaries in the world.

Soon a small, heavily loaded farm truck arrives, carrying a stupendous number of bright orange pumpkins. (One little girl exclaims "They're more than I can count!") The children and adults organize themselves into lines between the truck and CLEAR-WATER's gangplank, and a continuous procession of pumpkins begins bobbing along on their way to a temporary berth on the sloop's wide deck.

CLEARWATER carries a few basic props for her theatrical appearances: a small, portable microphone and amplifier; a folding billboard that explains the history of Hudson River sloops; and a little, painted wooden barrel to collect any spare quarters or paper money that visitors might consider uncomfortably heavy in their pockets. There are sometimes paper brochures to take home to your friends and neighbors. But the real souvenir is a glimpse of this American legend — a beautiful, wooden sailboat, her hard-working young crew, and this tireless old guy with his fisherman's cap and endless supply of folksongs.

CLEARWATER has inspired many other people to build large, traditional wooden sailing vessels, sometimes to perform similar educational work, but just as often simply for the hands-on sailing and boatbuilding experience that such a project offers. So it might be helpful to consider just how much boat we're talking about.

This is not a casual undertaking, and once you have launched a big, wooden sailboat like this, the really exhausting work of maintenance, repairs, crew training, and scheduling begins. It requires a small, full-time staff and a constant supply of volunteers, all of this backed by either a nonprofit organization or reliable, permanent corporate sponsors. Some wooden ships can actually pay their own way as charter vessels or sailing schools, but this often requires that they be home-ported in distant vacation-resort islands — that's where much of the charter business is, after all.

very long bowsprit make for a total length of 106 feet (32.3 meters). Total sail area is 4,305 square feet (400 square meters), the vast majority of it in that immense mainsail. But the surprise is that heavy main boom — 70 feet long (21.3 meters). It's almost as long as the boat itself, and must be jibed slowly across the deck with "complete respect."

Built of oak and fir at the Harvey Gamage Shipyard in Maine, CLEARWATER is true to her ancestors in every way, including the use of a very large centerboard to increase her draft from eigtht feet to 14 feet when water depth permits. With complete rig and normal ballast, the sloop weighs in at a displacement of 218,000 pounds.

The nuts and bolts of CLEARWATER's history reveal just how much of an accomplishment was her design, finance, and construction. Designed by Cyrus Hamlin, CLEARWATER was modeled conservatively after Hudson River sloops used between the American Revolution and the Civil War. Her wide hull alone is 76 feet (23.2 meters) long, and her maximum beam is 25 feet (7.6 meters) — almost exactly one-third her hull length! Bow and stern overhangs and that

Finally, with the wind and strong Hudson River tides to her advantage, CLEARWATER begins the long voyage south to Manhattan. Pete Seeger and the sloop crew pass the time "tuning up" — practicing songs while also doing minor repairs on deck. The boat sails through a few stretches of the deep river where signs of modern civilization are so rare that one feels transported back a century or two, and it wouldn't be surprising to see several other sloops coming around the next riverbend. The water is now much cleaner than it was a few decades ago, and both fish and other wildlife are returning.

The cargo of pumpkins reminds the CLEARWATER crew that they are about to do business with the hurried citizens of New York City. When the sloop eventually arrives at the historic South Street Seaport Museum on the southeast tip of Manhattan, she quickly ties up where clipper ships and wide-eyed immigrants once crowded the most famous waterfront in America. The pumpkins, colorful squash, and many one-gallon bottles of apple cider are unloaded and put on display. Soon a crowd of local urban natives appears, with chattering children in tow, and Pete Seeger steps up to the microphone. He introduces his motley band of lightning-fingered fellow musicians, he talks a little about how CLEARWATER needs public support and participation to continue her work, and he casts a spell at the dark sky to keep the threatening rain away for a few hours. Then the eerie twang of a banjo is heard echoing from city skyscrapers, and the grownups and kids are all singing a song they may have never heard before but will remember in the years to come.

To Be One

The builder name "Riva" is found on some of the most beautiful motor yachts in Europe, but that company's reputation started with fairly small motorboats designed originally for high-speed fun on high-altitude, freshwater Italian lakes. To me, the ultimate expression of Italian style and superb engineering may be a Ferrari racing car, or it may just as easily be the Riva "Super Aquarama" mahogany powerboat.

TO BE ONE is just one of many privately owned Rivas on the rocky Mediterranean coast, but this vessel does year 'round service as a water taxi in Portofino — arguably the prettiest and most expensive little "fishing village" resort in the world. Those big, ugly, white numerals are required by Italian customs on most vessels, especially any as fast and agile as a Riva, for the sensible reason that late-night offshore smuggling has a very old, honorable history on the Italian coastline.

However, TO BE ONE (named after a particularly hot disco song years ago) gets the same factory-authorized annual maintenance and expert varnishing as do those Super Aquaramas which never enter commercial service. All the original, voluptuous mahogany construction is in perfect shape — on deck, under water, and in the cockpit. It's unnerving to see that much flawless woodworking and glossy varnish in a boat which routinely carries baggage and big families between the waterfront and their yachts anchored offshore. But that's the life of a water taxi, and TO BE ONE's owner/operator can always disappear when necessary into the little cabin down below for a quick lunch and a nap.

Sailors sometimes use sophisticated electronics to keep track of how well their boat and sails are performing, but they can always just look up and instead "eyeball" the rig to get instant feed- back, assuming they know what to look for. Not so aboard a motor yacht — where only the vessel's speed and engine sounds give clues to the engine's health. If you need to keep track of how well a high-performance motor yacht is performing now and in the predictable future, you need a full array of instruments to measure and display subtle changes in the engine's behavior.

TO BE ONE has a full set of automotive-style instruments, but they are wrapped up and presented in one of the sexiest varnished-mahogany sculptures ever to be called a "dashboard." Lots of

what you see from the driver's seat is carved from solid mahogany planks, which are then joined and planed and sanded until they dissolve into the yacht's interior curves.

To me, the dark blue, crimson, and chrome interior of a "Team Warlock" 23-foot racing powerboat is just as beautiful, although certainly less comfortable, than what's aboard a Riva. The super-high-per-formance Warlock boat needs all the instrumentation possible, for even a few minutes' advance warning of engine problems can help to avoid disaster. While comparing these two very different vessels, it should be mentioned that the famous Riva boatyards also build some of the most high-tech, Star Wars-style motor yachts available, without one square centimeter of varnished wood in sight.

Solaria Too

When travelers to the South of France talk about the city of Cannes, they think of golden beaches, the world's smallest bathing suits, an opulent casino, and a lavish international film festival that makes Hollywood's Academy Awards "Oscar" ceremonies, in comparison, seem like a church social. Most visitors to Cannes would never expect to find a big, gray shipyard where people build military patrol boats and very large motor yachts. But on the west edge of Cannes there's just such a shipyard: Chantiers Navals de l'Estérel.

Here they can build the metal-alloy yachts and military vessels you might expect, but this

yard also specializes in solid-mahogany, laminated hulls — not because this is esthetically pleasing, but because laminated mahogany is, pound for pound, stronger and stiffer than either steel or aluminum. And the added hull thickness at equal weight means that a laminated-wood military vessel suffers less vibration and flexing while pushing the speed limit at sea. Skeptics who imagine that the increased flammability of wooden hulls is an issue here should remember two things: first, that fuel explosions cause most of the destruction in boat fires; and second, that the crew of a military vessel in today's hostile environments

would have absolutely no reason to care about fire hazard after their ship had already been vaporized by a missile.

Missiles, luckily, are not expected aboard the all-mahogany SOLARIA TOO, a 26-meter twin-engine Estérel motor yacht built for an English owner. The high-tech style evident on deck and down below is instead intended for carefree family vacations and cocktail parties, with an occasional break for sunbathing. Removable plush cushions can be stowed below deck when necessary, and an impressively handsome "push-button" forward hatch opens to allow direct access to private living quarters.

One of the distinguishing characteristics of yacht interior design is the need to "round off" all corners and edges, to compensate for the increased risk of soft human bodies hitting sharp corners in the confined spaces below deck. Aboard something as roomy as SOLARIA TOO, that risk might not seem so great, and it's tempting to build cabinetry in styles more appropriate in homes ashore. But any seagoing vessel, especially one as fast as SOLARIA TOO, will eventually cross another ship's wake or meet rough weather, and her passengers may get rattled around.

SOLARIA TOO combines extremely modern, streamlined furniture design with an extremely hard wood known as Afrormosia. Corners and edges are rounded in whatever dimension is appropriate: downward along the front of cabinets, or horizontally in doorways and tight hallways. To match the resulting look and feel of all these quarter- and half-round

wood edges, and to create handholds which actually feel good in your hands, other components, such as drawer pulls, are made of simple wooden cylinders. Anyone familiar with the beautiful Art Deco style variation known as "Steamship Deco" will recognize this simplified use of circles and cylinders. A more subtle reason for round port-lights and other hull openings, along with rounded deck hatches and bulkhead doors, is that an opening in a structural panel is much more likely to develop cracks at sharp, square corners.

Sometimes the interplay between circles, cylinders, and square edges aboard SOLARIA TOO is just for decorative purposes. Most of the doorknobs are simple cylinder sections, framed by waterproof, colorful fabrics. All of these components are selected for their maxi-mum resistance to salt corrosion, even when they are located deep within the yacht's dry interior.

Californian

Using the word "yacht" to describe CALIFORNIAN might seem a bit exaggerated, unless one remembers the historic origins of the word: Seventeenth century English and Dutch royalty believed that yachting required miniature warships, complete with cannons, large crews, and lavish accommodations. CALIFORNIAN is a recreation of the 1849 revenue cutter LAWRENCE, a fast and seaworthy vessel with which the United States Revenue Service (today's Coast Guard) once patrolled the dangerous California coast during the Gold Rush.

There is no doubt, however, of CALIFORNIAN's status today as a busy passenger-charter vessel. This 94-foot topsail schooner, besides being the official Tallship Ambassador of the California State Legislature, routinely carries hundreds of paying adults and teenagers on a wide variety of deepwater cruises, sailing from Southern California to British Columbia, and even Hawaii. CALIFORNIAN is special not only for its historic design and traditional construction, but also because the ship was the first large sail-training vessel to operate along California's beautiful, rugged coastline.

Available both to members of the sponsoring Nautical Heritage Society (based in Dana Point, California) and to the general public are several types of coastal cruises and longer ocean passages. There are "daysails" for as many as 40 adults; one-day cruises are either part of CALIFORNIAN's regular schedule or special events arranged with advance notice. There are also extended "High Seas Adventure" cruises for 12 adult passengers, as well as shorter "Coastal Cadet" cruises for 12 students at a time. "Special Cadet" cruises take 12 students on extended voyages, often as far away as Hawaii.

Students (ages 16 to 25) on the cadet cruises are taught and certified by all eight professional officers/ crew of CALIFORNIAN; certificates are recognized by the American Sail Training Association and other organizations. Although many individuals, groups, and corporations provide CALIFORNIAN with tax-deductible donations, supplies, and services, the simplest way to support the non-profit Nautical Heritage Society (and to stay informed of their ship's future schedule) is the Society's modest membership fee. Separately, students should ask for the Sea Cadet brochure, application, and schedule.

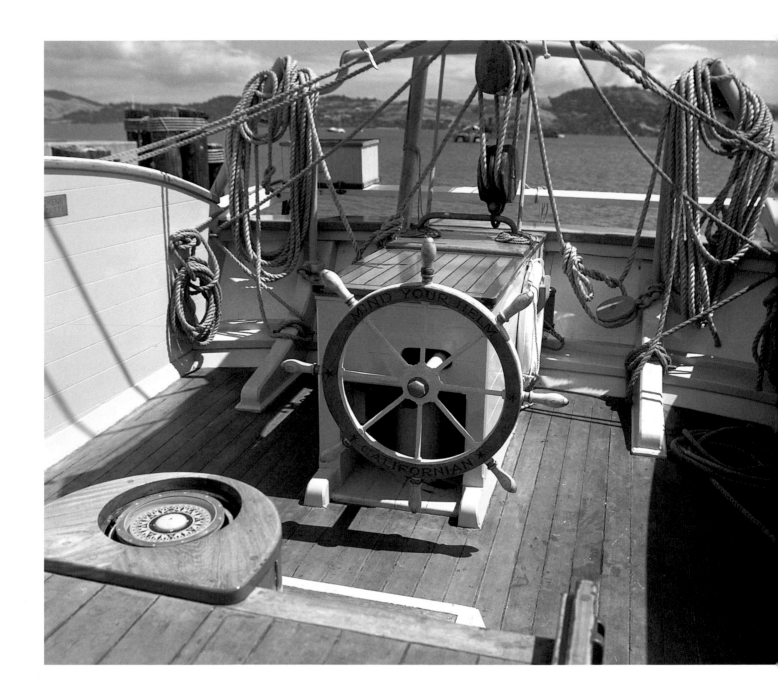

CALIFORNIAN was designed by Melbourne Smith of Annapolis, Maryland, and built by him along with members, employees, and volunteers of the Nautical Heritage Society. The vessel was launched in 1984 in San Diego, California. The vessel's facts and features are as follows: length overall/sparred, 145 feet; length on deck, 93 feet, 6 inches; length waterline, 83 feet; beam, maximum, 24 feet, 6 inches; draft, 9 feet, 6 inches; and displacement, 13 long tons. Sail area is 7,000 square feet with all topsails set,

and auxiliary power is a 100-horsepower diesel. Construction is all wood, planked on laminated frames and beams.

Accommodations for cadet and adult cruises (apart from the "Governor's Cabin" saloon seen here) are enclosed Pullman bunks, shared bathroom, and the ship's main saloon. The separate Governor's Cabin suite (private saloon, two staterooms, galley, head) is also available — for two adult couples only — during cadet cruises. For Very Important Passengers, one of the first

subtle indications that the elegant Governor's Cabin saloon is somewhat different from their usual hotel suites is that heavy furniture is securely bolted to the floorboards or cabin walls. Large sailing vessels, unlike hotels, are expected to heel over in strong winds, so wandering furniture and loose cannons are discouraged.

Operating a vessel this size and with this much authentic, traditional rigging requires a veteran, professional crew and captain. As always, the heart of the ship is the helm, in this case a ship's wheel made of iron and wood, with a big mariner's compass directly forward. Here is where some crewmember or young cadet will stand for hours, dutifully minding the helm while the hair on the back of his head is warmed by the captain's stern gaze. CALIFORNIAN has two large storage compartments on her aft deck; these low, permanent structures offer some protection for the helm in heavy weather and keep extra passenger life jackets quickly accessible.

Assuming that you, dear reader, have not yet been aboard a large, traditional, wooden sailing vessel when it was, in fact, sailing, then I'd like to recommend highly that you try it. No matter how much you know about the history of human migration across oceans, and no matter how many movies you've seen with various pirates swashbuckling and hoisting their mizzens and otherwise getting all wet, you cannot imagine what it feels like to have a big, wooden ship carrying your precious bottom safely suspended over the deep, blue sea. The physical experience is unique, rather like standing aboard an immense friendly whale which politely cruises only at the water's surface, providing you with a soft, roller coaster ride through wild waves and storms.

You quickly become "attached" to your ship. You may even call it "she" or "her" when you start to feel the maternal protection which ships have always given their frail, dependent passengers. If you're cold, hungry, or wet, or if you find yourself at sea at night with the full moon and stars high overhead, you may even think about ancient sailors who passed this way before you, and how they felt about being "waterborne" in their floating wooden cradles, or about the mysterious, unseen forces which launched our little, moist planet into time and space.

Or you can simply think of it as sailing aboard a wooden ship, if you prefer. Aboard the topsail schooner CALIFORNIAN, one of the forceful reminders that her particular ancestors were truly warships is that full-size, fully-operational cannons (normally unloaded) are part of the schooner's regular equipment. They occasionally serve as temporary extra benches for visiting passengers during CALIFORNIAN's many goodwill and diplomatic tours to distant ports.

Groote Beer

The Great Bear (Ursus Major) constellation is just one of many designs carved into the wooden beams aboard GROOTE BEER. Down below, there are seashells, seahorses, crabs, fishes, dolphins, birds, the sun, and of course voluptuous mermaids parading across the overhead panels and structural members. The entire interior, and even many of the exterior deck structures, aboard this traditional North Sea "botterjacht" are a living testament to the creative skills of Netherlands boatbuilders and woodcarvers long ago.

Those skills may have helped to keep those old boatbuilders alive. One legend says that, because GROOTE BEER was built during World War II, supposedly for a wealthy Nazi officer (possibly even Adolf Hitler's Air Marshal Hermann Goering), the Dutch boatbuilders and carvers employed on this project were temporarily exempt from conscription into Nazi labor camps. So it was a "good idea" for these old men to do a good job, in fact an exceptionally good job, with their carving, not merely to please their dangerous client but to keep the job in progress as long as humanly possible — preferably until the war ended.

GROOTE BEER was completed in 1945 at the J. Kok Shipyard in Huizen, the Netherlands. Her interior was completed by H.W. DeVoogt & Zoon, Haarlem. Despite this vessel's rather cheerful, even "cute" appearance and appealing traditional rig, the truth is that she is a big, heavy brute: 67 feet overall length; 52 feet, 6 inches length on deck; and displacement of 83,752 pounds. The barge-shaped GROOTE BEER's normal draft is a mere four feet until she lowers her leeboards and draws a full 10 feet. The vessel is perfect for sailing in shallow, coastal waters and the famous Holland canals.

GROOTE BEER is also a perfect family cruiser, if you can get over the fact that her cozy interior feels like a priceless museum devoted to master woodworking. That museum quality brings me to one important warning about the "charm" of large, wooden classics: This vessel was built in an era when labor (and sometimes life itself) was considered cheap, so little thought was given to the yacht's ease of maintenance or repair. The only way to keep GROOTE BEER's amazing interior in good shape nowadays is to spend serious time and money on fre-quent haulouts, forced-air ventilation, expert varnishing, and only the very best repair work. A large family of dedicated woodworkers and meticulous do-it-yourselfers could cope with GROOTE BEER's upkeep, but any other owners had better be ready for some substantial boatyard invoices.

That said, it should also be obvious that nothing you see below deck aboard this yacht couldn't be imitated, and maybe even improved upon, in a new wooden yacht. The same flamboy-ant carving style could be followed up with a deep, penetrating oil finish or a

super- durable synthetic varnish. GROOTE BEER's fairly ponderous fireplace design is just fine aboard a large vessel modeled after traditional cargo barges, but a lighter design could use the same Delft tile without a massive marble base. You get the idea. Likewise, keep in mind that the woodworking seen here was done before modern goodies like waterproof marine plywood were available; a clever boatbuilder today could easily match GROOTE BEER's interior style, but without the weight and massive construction required.

Back to that woodcarving. Today, in our pre-fabricated, machine-made world, the only way to get woodcarving this good is to hunt through all the advertisements in your favorite wooden-boat magazine, and then locate a really experienced master carver in your area (a true "shipcarver" is best but not always necessary). Or you could do the carving yourself. Just be sure to read up and practice a lot on wooden objects of lesser value before attacking your boat interior. Try out your carving aptitude on an old chair, or maybe the inside of a closet door. When your skills are better developed and you can transform a

block of hard, seasoned oak into a writhing, realistic sea serpent (without stabbing yourself with the chisel), then load up your tools and head for the boatyard. By then you'll also appreciate just how much work and expertise went into GROOTE BEER's astounding interior.

One item aboard this yacht always catches the attention of woodworkers and furniture-design aficionados. The cabinet top surfaces are made of tightly-woven wood strips supported by a rigid, seamless wooden framework and then saturated with many, many coats of clear varnish. How many? "Enough to make the surface perfectly flat and smooth, with the wood strips well protected." This response comes from a yachtbuilder friend who duplicated this woven-strip construction. "Use heavy-duty spar varnish or some clear, ultra-hard synthetic which allows multiple layers, and let it dry evenly and slowly. Count on a few weeks before it looks good. Be patient." Another caveat: Invisible repairs to a woven-strip wooden surface are either nearly impossible or not worth it, depending on your level of ambition. Don't install something as tricky and valuable as this type of wooden surface if you plan to drop wrenches or cutlery on your creation.

Nuovo Aiuto Di Dio

Many Italians couldn't care less about anything traditional and old-fashioned. Think of it from their point of view. Maybe it comes from living in a country where every hill and house foundation probably contains a few ancient Roman artifacts. You could easily grow up with a strong preference for modern architecture, high-tech, fast cars, and T.V. shows about invaders from outer space.

This might explain the reaction I got when poking around the Ligurian coast of Italy, for I asked several waterfront folks where I might find and photograph some "traditional Italian sailing yachts." The most common answer was "Why do you need this for? We have much better modern yachts." But I persevered in my quest, and finally I met an old fisherman who pointed down into a small bay surrounded by steep, green hillsides, and there at a mooring waited NUOVO AIUTO DI DIO ("New Aide of God"). I had stumbled upon one of the very last traditional, lateen-rigged cargo vessels in Italy. Built in 1925, this lute-shaped "liuto" had a hull and rig design that dates back thousands of years.

NUOVO AIUTO DI DIO hauled just about anything that Mediterranean commerce required, but her normal cargo was wine barrels. Offloaded into the surf or on small stone piers in seaside villages, the heavy barrels were rolled up the beach by the very people who would soon consume the barrels' precious contents. So the liuto hull was very shallow: NUOVO is 50 feet long on deck, but draws onlly three feet when partly loaded. (A working liuto with a truly heavy load often had its deck awash for most of a voyage.) That very long bowsprit takes the overall/sparred length up to 71 feet.

Modern sailboats are designed for a very wide range of conditions, but they generally have round, pointy-ended hulls with nearly flat decks. Getting accustomed to that sort of hull and deck environment means that one's first steps aboard NUOVO AIUTO DI DIO are very disorienting; here is a vintage working sailboat hull (fully restored and with a sensible, yachty interior added) which is shaped exactly like the wine barrels it once carried aboard! The center of a liuto's broad deck is a safe place to stand, but careless steps near the outer edges can take you rolling down into the water. The sensation could be compared to riding a very determined swimming pig — one who carries a huge, slanted, wooden cross with triangular Egyptian-cotton sails.

None of the sail-handling gear aboard NUOVO AIUTO DI DIO bears a strong resemblance to any of the modern or even traditional rigs I had seen in American or Northern European sailboats. The lateen (Latin) rig is a very ancient mast-and-spar system with roots in Mediterranean, Egyptian, and East African history. It is actually simple, fast, efficient, and, at least in light airs, not too complicated to handle. But aboard a liuto contending with a heavy load and howling Mediterranean storms, that immense "antenna" spar and "vela latina" mainsail are unruly monsters.

Thus, carrying an anchor of respectable size and weight was a good plan aboard any working liuto — to protect her crew and sacred liquid cargo. Note the impressive anchor carried aboard NUOVO AIUTO DI DIO; this mighty iron hook is just the thing for keeping off a rocky shore when fickle winds threaten. An anchor is too heavy only if the crew can't handle it, but an anchor that's too light is the worst form of bad luck.

Unicorn

Of all the well-traveled, weather-beaten wooden sailing vessels in the world, few have accumulated more mileage and salty tales than has the brig UNICORN. Launched in 1948 in Sibbo, Finland, the schooner originally named LYRA spent a long career hauling lumber, sand, and other bulk cargoes to Finnish cities damaged during World War II. In 1972, a French-American professional photographer named Jacques Thiry and Finnish shipwright Pertti Tarvas saved what was left of LYRA and rebuilt her in Sweden — where prime timber and skilled labor are plentiful.

Using plans from the 1867 French brig ADOLPH & LAURA, Thiry's small band of boatbuilders and sailors transformed LYRA into the newly baptized UNICORN, which soon sailed to England, Spain, and then across the Atlantic to Bermuda. For years, UNICORN scraped together a precarious living by hauling small cargoes and a few passengers between Caribbean islands. But Hurricane Fifi (and a famous 30-ton cargo of bananas rotting before delivery) blew away Jacques Thiry's dream for his own wooden sailing ship — one that earned its way as a working vessel.

Soon UNICORN was in Florida, and she was saved by the late multi-millionaire William W. Smith, who had also saved the 177-foot Portuguese barkentine GAZELA PRIMEIRO. Completely overhauled at Robert Derecktor's Fort Lauderdale boatyard, UNICORN had absorbed a cool million dollars of Smith's

wealth but was ready for a 1976 *Operation Sail Tall Ships* appearance at America's Bicentennial festivities in New York Harbor. Last I saw her, UNICORN had a very professional crew and was owned by a nonprofit organization dedicated to full-time charter work and educational programs for schoolchildren. The old Finnish schooner LYRA, nearly lost before being resurrected as the brig UNICORN, was now helping wide-eyed city kids to "learn the ropes."

Some history, facts, and figures about the brig UNICORN will help to explain why creating such a complex, remarkable vessel required the efforts and contributions of so many people. Designed and built in 1948 by Helge Johansson in Sibbo, Finland, the schooner LYRA was a practical, heavy cargo vessel without any frills. The hull was 96 feet long on deck, displaced 551,000 pounds (or more if the cargo was substantial), and had a maximum beam of 24 feet.

By the time LYRA was re-named UNICORN and had survived all the way to the 1976 *Operation Sail Tall Ships* appearance in New York, the new vessel had acquired an entirely new rig, including flax squaresails, fore/aft sails, and even studding sails (with a grand total sail area of over 7,000 square feet). She had a rebuilt hull, a new 335-horsepower diesel engine, new interior bulkheads (to strengthen the hull and allow U.S. Coast Guard passenger-vessel certification) and, most importantly, a large family of volunteers and a paid, professional crew to keep her healthy.

Much of UNICORN's success is due to the many volunteers who offered specific woodworking skills or other projects as their contributions. Sometimes that means a new deck hatch, or a table in the crew's mess, or even some custom metal-forging and castings. The involvement of a local community (in UNICORN's case, the residents of Tampa, Florida) seems to be the secret ingredient, even when many volunteers have never done any sailing in their lives.

Blue Peter

Traditionally, ships and yachts on the eve of departure before a voyage would hoist a special blue-and-white flag called "the Blue Peter." As I understand it, this English/American flag name derives from the ancient French phrase "bleu partir." One very good reason H.W. McCurdy named his 96-foot yacht after this historic flag is that McCurdy is part of that very small percentage of yacht owners whose vessels actually leave the dock — at nearly every opportunity.

I first heard about BLUE PETER, and then saw this vessel, after I strolled through the elegant Seattle Yacht Club on a hot summer day. I was lucky enough to "consult" with the bartender and a few of his knowledgable older customers, so I asked them if any big power yachts, preferably wooden classics, might be lurking out there under the surrounding big, shady trees. I was especially interested in finding yachts which best represent classic boatbuilding in the Northwest United States. This last specification prompted my consultants to look at each other, carefully set down their gin-and-tonics, and confidently proclaim "You absolutely must see BLUE PETER."

So I did, after Mr. McCurdy stopped by the club and offered an informal tour of his big, powerful yacht. (With twin 330-horsepower diesel engines, this vessel could easily serve as a tugboat in emergencies.) I discovered that "Mac" had grown up working at various watery occupations in nearby, historic Port Townsend, Washington, and could remember seeing dozens of big squareriggers waiting for cargoes of lumber, grain, and salmon. But it was many years later, during a break while attending the Massachusetts Institute of Technology, that he glimpsed the famous millionaires' yachts off Marblehead and determined to earn enough so that he, too, could afford an elegant live-aboard yacht.

BLUE PETER adds new meaning to the phrase "Army surplus." After World War II, McCurdy purchased his future yacht after its long service as a U.S. Army vessel, and he supervised her renovation in his shipyard. Nearly all of the superb interior now seen aboard BLUE PETER was first installed or rebuilt at that time. Since then, a few decades of constant attention and improvement have polished up the interior and "put everything in its proper place." You can open any drawer, look under any floorboard, or conduct the most intense inspection of the engine compartment, and you will find that nothing's missing and eveything's where it ought to be. That's what they call "shipshape" — an excellent thing for a ship to be when crew safety depends on knowing exactly where tools and equipment are when you'll need them.

BLUE PETER combines solid efficiency, elegance, and simplicity. All that brass, mahogany, and teak in the yacht's interior is designed not just to look good, but to withstand many years of contact with

water, salt, and (worst of all) the oils and chemicals left by human contact. The only "maintenance" required for nearly all of that fancy cabinetry is a regular wipe with plain water. Cabins aboard BLUE PETER smell clean and fresh, due to the constant, plentiful ventilation that was specified during the yacht's original construction. Even with all portlights and hatches sealed tightly, fresh air flows naturally, or with help from electric blowers, through the hidden structure of this wooden hull.

Cherokee

Most yacht owners do a good job of getting just their immediate family and a few friends aboard for the occasional weekend cruise. Ann Sutter and her 26-foot classic CHEROKEE have done a great job of introducing hundreds of people to the relaxed art of recreational yachting. Sausalito, California is home port for the restored wooden CHEROKEE, but this popular little craft always seems to be at the center of weekend picnic cruises, classic yacht parades, and group tours of San Francisco Bay.

Although there's a cozy little sleeping cabin in the forward part of this little yacht, CHEROKEE's usual mission is simply day-long cruises to explore the waterfront and enjoy wine and nibbles. Sometimes the only reason for a cruise is to venture out and confirm that the Golden Gate Bridge is still standing where it should be, after which CHEROKEE toodles slowly back to Sausalito. At other times, this determined little yacht heads up the Sacramento, San Joaquin, and Petaluma Rivers, all of which feed into San Francisco Bay.

What's impressive is that Ann Sutter paid just $900 for CHEROKEE before restoration, which included lengthening the cabin structure, installing the forward bunk, and adding amenities such as a gravity-fed fresh-water supply (see that little tank on the cabin roof?) The basic hull was in good shape and was lucky to have bronze portholes and fittings. Then came goodies such as a great stereo system, a little toilet, and a well-stocked winerack. Guests aboard CHEROKEE are often first-time boaters, but they quickly relax with Ann at the helm. By the end of the cruise, these guests are often talking about boating or sailing classes — anything to get back on the water.

Ming Hai

If you'd really like to expand your boating horizons, not merely on the water but between your ears, buy a copy of the book *Junk's and Sampans of the Yangtze*, by G.R.G. Worcester. This is one of several great books which would help the North American or European sailor to understand just how deep is China's maritime tradition. I mention all this just in case the reader hears the phrase "Chinese junk" and then imagines a slow, heavy barge with barely enough sail area to navigate Hong Kong Harbor. Long before European sailors began to leave safe coastal waters, their counterparts in ancient China were boldly sailing huge seagoing junks to India and Africa. They may even have sailed to North and Central America, but that's a subject for another time.

The 50-foot MING HAI ("Clear and Bright Seas") is perhaps a bit domesticated as far as junks go, but she has taken many a deep-water cruise, including at least one 2,000-mile tour of the Caribbean. Last I saw this solid-teak, Hong Kong-built live-aboard, she was serving as a floating Florida home for ex-Central Intelligence Agency officer Joe Maggio and his family. Author of the book *Company Man*, Maggio bought MING HAI during the yacht's construction and had her shipped across the Pacific Ocean. Her admittedly untraditional wheelhouse and oversize main cabin add a tremendous amount of interior space, and that colorful interior is as cozy and comfortable as any luxury hotel suite.

A guy who has worked for the U.S. Central Intelligence Agency probably needs a highly developed sense of humor. Aboard MING HAI, that includes Joe Maggio's copy of Mao Tse-Tung's famous "little red book" of political wisdom (unfortunately not autographed by the late Chinese Communist leader). Then there's that cheerful little panda pillow and various exotic memorabilia from travels long ago in Southeast Asia.

But MING HAI is also very well equipped with completely efficient, practical things like a full kitchen and gas range/oven, a large-capacity fresh-water system, and excellent heating and ventilation. When the time comes to visit another port, MING HAI can fire up her Mercedes-Benz 150-horsepower diesel, or her three "lug-rigged," fully-battened sails can move this heavy yacht along at

a decent speed — considering that this is one lucky family's completely-furnished live-aboard home. Standard operating procedure for guests and permanent residents on this yacht is to go barefoot whenever possible, mostly to keep the many woven rugs aboard as clean as possible.

Also, that bright, yellow-fabric canopy over nearly the entire deck and cabin creates a casual "second floor" of usable living space in Florida's warm climate. In the evening, nothing beats sitting on the wide aft deck while listening to the manatees and seabirds slowly circling the yacht. The canopy overhead protects against afternoon rain, as well as the midday sun, so Florida's everchanging climate becomes simply a welcome part of life aboard this yacht.

Sunrise

The world of sailing-yacht design is, in general, divided cleanly into distinct boat categories: traditionally-rigged woodies; sleek, high-tech racers; fiberglass family cruisers; ultralight "downhill sleds"; multi-hulls; and so on. Each category has many variations within it. And there's a very sensible reason for all these major and minor variations. There is no single yacht design that's "ideal" for all conditions, so designers wrestle with their clients and their conscience until the future yacht fits its intended purpose.

Unfortunately, that also means that both designers and yacht owners are often too cautious about combining attributes from different types of boats. Some traditionalists follow tradition blindly, and many modernists blindly pay for all sorts of high-tech sails and equipment that really make sense aboard only the most extreme racing boats (if they make sense at all). All this can make for some frustrated families and guests when a yacht design places greater emphasis on popular convention than on ease of use.

So, with all that said, I should also mention that some yacht designers have the technical skills and historic perspective necessary to combine the best of traditional and modern yacht design. Jay Benford and his famous little live-aboard SUNRISE impressed me because of that versatility.

SUNRISE is a traditional "pinky" ketch, 50 feet overall and 38 feet long on deck. Her divided rig spreads a lot of sail area fore-and-aft, which is less "efficient" aerodynamically than a single sail that's very tall, until you consider that the lower, longer rig with separate sails is often much easier to handle and to keep aloft when the wind pipes up. SUNRISE carries two square sails on her main mast, and these old-fashioned things deliver amazing power while being surprisingly easy to manage. Benford has specified square sails in some of his cruising designs, yet he surprises hard-core traditionalists by sometimes specifying a modern, roller-furling system for those sails.

The term "pinky" has very ancient linguistic roots from Mediterranean maritime history, and possibly from points farther east. It refers to that long, pointed stern overhang above the rudder. The long stern structure has many advantages at sea, especially for fishing boats using nets, for sail handling, and when a convenient outdoor toilet is required.

I'm one of those old-timers who has an unbroken, complete collection of *Wooden Boat Magazine* issues, going back all the way to the charter issue #1 (September/October 1974). Many of those issues of *Wooden Boat* have big color advertisements for the trademarked "Deks Olje" clear-oil system from Norway. Those ads frequently show the pinky ketch SUNRISE sailing along, with her stem-to-stern Deks Olje finish sparkling in the sun. Those were very effective ads, although getting up close and personal with SUNRISE's clear finish and impeccable woodworking is even better. But there's no "decoration" here — what you see is 100 percent functional, even if it is damned pretty.

A very important part of many traditional sailing vessels is the old-fashioned "pinrail" and "fiferail." These wooden or iron rails

had socket-holes whose function was to hold long metal or hardwood belaying-pins (normally removable for special occasions such as pirate attacks), to which were secured all the many ropes used to raise, lower, and trim sails, spars, and pennants. Designing these massive pinrails didn't require much artistic sense, only a perfect grasp of structural engineering. For example, if all those halyards and ropes are pulling upward in unison, then logically a pinrail must be strong enough not to break and not to detach from the deck below. Throughout yachting history, many a lovely little varnished pinrail has exploded straight up into the sky because of careless construction; its replacement normally has less finicky varnish, is no longer so little, and often includes some thick bronze rods to connect invisibly through the deck.

Dauntless and Scirocco

John Alden, who designed some very famous sailing yachts for some very rich and famous clients, clearly had a knack for combining speed and elegance. The staysail schooner DAUNTLESS, at 61 feet length on deck (74 feet overall), was built in 1930 and has been lovingly maintained by a series of owners, some of whom were willing and able to sprinkle substantial sums of money on restoring this floating masterpiece. DAUNT-LESS has also done some serious sailing and racing, including a few wild rides through 40-knot fog on San Francisco Bay. (Yes, I was extremely wet and weightless while photographing this yacht in the 1981 Master Mariners Regatta.)

The schooner's long list of past destinations includes the coasts of Florida, Mexico, South America, and many Caribbean islands. Along the way, DAUNTLESS has had her hull rebuilt and her interior repeatedly redesigned. That colorful interior is "unfaithful" to the original design in many ways, except for the careful use of top-quality hardwoods and solid-brass fittings for all new construction.

If you take a close look, for example, at a deck hatch aboard DAUNT-LESS, you start to understand why this old wooden classic remains valuable (it's not merely the John Alden name). From down below, the deck hatch is opened or locked tightly shut with superbly machined hardware. On deck, that same hatch is designed to withstand strong winds, water seepage, and the routine traffic of humans, ropes, and equipment. The hatch must offer a low profile so that it doesn't easily snag ropes or damage tender knees and shins of passing crewmembers. Above all, the hatch, when closed, must never leak, so construction techniques which are adequate for "weatherproof" window frames in your house are nowhere near adequate in a sailboat hatch. It's not the purpose of this book to teach boatbuilding, but I would like to remind future yacht owners that many tired, homesick crewmembers have completely lost their minds and "jumped ship" simply because of slow, constant drip-drip-drips over their bunks.

Comparing the interiors aboard the schooner DAUNTLESS and the Alden- designed, 74-foot cutter SCIROCCO is instructive. DAUNTLESS has been the pride and joy of some fun-loving owners who indulged their preference for lively colors and bold design. SCIROCCO was in the Caribbean charter trade when I saw her, and so her owners had retained a more traditional style of upholstery and allowed only a few interior changes (like installing a waterproof stereo-speaker housing overhead).

This reverence for SCIROCCO's past might have something to do with one of her early, very famous, owners. Launched with a ketch rig in 1929, the yacht was soon bought by the flamboyant movie star Errol Flynn. He then captained the vessel from New York, through the Caribbean and the Panama Canal, all the way around to California. SCIROCCO became a warm favorite among Flynn's Hollywood party crowd, and that's when his luck ran out. A young woman accused Flynn of statutory rape, allegedly committed while she attended one of the many notorious parties aboard his yacht. Lurid newspaper head-lines and a heated court trial ensued, and it all led to nothing except Flynn's failed marriage and the go-get-'em popular phrase "in like Flynn." If you care to read all about it, get the book *Bring On the Empty Horses*, written by Flynn's fellow movie idol David Niven. Or you could go straight to the source and read Flynn's autobiography, *My Wicked, Wicked Ways.*

Whatever luck Flynn had playing at various games of chance, he apparently had superb taste in yacht design. SCIROCCO was a thoroughbred from the very first, and she was sailed constantly even after Flynn sold the yacht in the early 1940s. In 1969, a new owner began a seven-year circumnavigation, which took the vessel to Tahiti, Madagascar, South Africa, and Brazil — with a complete renovation in New Zealand. That's where she acquired the simple cutter rig, while keeping her classic mahogany interior.

Eilean

Saint Thomas in the U.S. Virgin Islands is one of the busiest centers of year 'round yacht chartering in the world. On any given day, you can walk along a commercial dock in Charlotte Amalie Harbor and see at least a few dozen of the most beautiful sailing and motor yachts in the Caribbean. Most of them will be filling up their fuel and water tanks, exchanging loads of dirty and clean laundry, and welcoming the next group of charter passengers. The vessels you see at any one time are only a tiny subset among the hundreds of yachts which call this their home port.

Among all these vessels, I happened to spot the 73-foot ketch EILEAN. I had put away my cameras and was strolling off to have dinner, all the while enjoying the Caribbean breeze and an awe-inspiring sunset. But pure luck took me past the charter dock where EILEAN had ghosted in and tied up, and I ventured forth to ask if her master and crew wouldn't mind a few photos taken aboard this classic Scots-built ketch. The captain turned out to be a quiet, calm young Frenchman wearing a nearly nonexistent bathing suit, but his attention was completely distracted by the need to soothe a red-haired, wildly freckled young American woman who threatened to quit his crew and his life forever. EILEAN would berth at that dock only for the night and early morning, leaving soon after sunrise, so any pictures I took had to be taken overnight. Perhaps this tight schedule had something to do with relations between captain and crew.

In any event, while hasty diplomatic progress was made ashore by our intrepid Frenchman, I slowly perused EILEAN's scrapbook, which contained faded newspaper clippings and magazine articles, along with original drawings and builder's certificates. I learned that EILEAN was designed and built by the famous William Fife, Jr., in Fairlie, Scotland, and launched in 1937. Knowing a little bit about boatbuilding, I was amazed to discover that this ketch was built with Burma teak hull and deck planks over steel frames, fastened with insulated phosphor-bronze bolts. This same "composite" construction (which can lead to nasty problems with metal corrosion when carelessly applied) was used with great success in the famous clipper ship CUTTY SARK.

M any classic British and Scottish sail- ing yachts, especially oceangoing vessels, which must endure heavy weather, are relatively narrow and deep, their designers having wisely decided in favor of seakeeping qualities at the expense of interior volume. A long, narrow hull like EILEAN's is therefore rather like a long submarine. There's room aboard for you, your passengers, and your gear, but they are aligned a lot differently than would be the case in a hull with greater beam. The benefit of this elongated, heavy hull becomes apparent only when its passengers glide serenely over waves which would make fat, lightweight sailboats uncomfortably bouncy. While EILEAN has adequate natural light coming in through deck hatches, the deck openings are relatively small and discreet, allowing for ventilation but protecting charter guests from the hot Caribbean sun.

EILEAN's main cabin is designed both as a comfortable, quiet compartment and also necessarily as a passageway between one end of the ship and the other. Deep carpet (take your dirty shoes off!) makes the interior very quiet. A gimbaled, folding table allows for complete dinner settings or after-dinner board games, with room left over for whatever ancient Scots refreshment may be appropriate.

Bunks and cabinets aboard EILEAN are of oak and teak construction, and every available extra cubic centimeter of interior space has been used for storage. Some design details here are worthy of mention: Bunks have hinged sides that can be lowered when necessary; sliding drawers have hidden latches to prevent accidental opening when at sea; and all the natural-color oak cabinetry shows relatively simple grain with no bold patterns, so the overall appearance is warm but understated.

Javeline

I visited JAVELINE on the exact day when this 75-foot, gaff-rigged, English ketch was getting itself and its heavy anchors extricated from a crowded marina in Cannes, France. New owner Emyr W. Davies had hired some skilled local divers to untangle an anchor and chain which had been on the muddy bottom for years, with the ketch itself getting almost as little use. A complete bottom scraping, survey, and repainting was in order, but at least the majority of this 100-year-old yacht's interior was in almost original condition. The teak-on-oak hull was in good shape, and all her massive gear on deck simply needed lots of scraping and paint. Not easy, but certainly not impossible.

One unique aspect of a large, heavy classic vessel built this well is that an owner gets to enjoy traditional deck details which today are assumed to be too expensive to imitate — and may be out of the question anyway aboard modern, lightweight hulls. JAVELINE boasts some deck construction which serves double duty: One large hatch, in particular, functions both as a comfortable passenger bench and as a waterproof, illuminating

deck hatch with large glass panels at its base. (These get cracked over the course of many decades but are easily replaced.)

JAVELINE's interior also shows many traditional values at their best. Knowing that, over time, humans and their monkeyish hands will scratch and stain any fine woodworking, especially around doorknobs and keyholes, JAVELINE's builders were generous in their use of decorative brass escutcheons to protect the wood below. The brass has surface designs which make this antique hardware even more historically valuable.

The ketch JAVELINE was launched (as JAVELIN, I might add) by her designer/builder Summers & Payne, Ltd., Southampton, England, in the year 1897. She displaces a hefty 154,280 pounds (70,000 kilograms), with a waterline length of 56 feet. Her substantial bowsprit gives her an overall length of 85 feet, and all of that can be driven briskly along in heavy weather by 3,100 square feet of sail.

Below deck, cabinetry details reveal the elegant secrets of classic yacht design, but also how decades of neglect can almost ruin a yacht's original interior. JAVELINE's drawer pulls, made of finely cast brass, had been polished vigorously with some unknown abrasive liquid, yet at the obvious expense of surrounding wood. The preferred technique is either to leave well enough alone (rather like the medical admonition "First, do no harm") or to completely remove the brass hardware and polish it well away from the wooden drawers — which could during the interval be sanded or chemically stripped, and then revarnished.

Some cabins aboard JAVELINE have narrow shelves with delicate wood-and-brass rails to keep small objects reasonably secure when the yacht is sailing. In a decent storm, even these small items would get stowed safely away. Above the shelves are small brass vents which let air circulate up and down along the hull's wooden frames, hidden there behind the interior panels. These vents appear to be mere decorations to most visiting guests, but the longevity of JAVELINE's hull can be credited to hundreds of subtle details like the vents, along with builder's tricks now hidden deep in the yacht's original construction.

X e b e c

The "steam yacht" XEBEC was designed by Charles Nicholson and built in 1900 by Camper & Nicholson, Ltd., Gosport, England. This 115-foot vessel was constructed of Burma teak plank bronze-riveted on oak frames, with her original power coming from a two-cylinder, coal-fired steam engine, along with 1,000 square feet of auxiliary sail. XEBEC was looked after by many owners, but her last owners had both the good fortune to live for many years aboard her, as well as the misfortune to witness their priceless yacht's destruction by a Caribbean hurricane. Much of their life savings had gone into maintaining and repairing XEBEC, as had many years of tender, loving care.

I was honored with the opportunity to photograph this nearly unique vessel in the U.S. Virgin Islands. The experience can be fairly compared to a time warp, for at one moment I was in the "real" world of jumbo jets, television sets, instant cameras, and the Internet, and suddenly I was transported back many decades — finding myself aboard a little ship which quite literally belonged in English history books. Only a few anachronisms aboard — a radio playing modern music, a recent newspaper on a table — reminded this visitor that XEBEC had not miraculously floated back to the beginning of England's Industrial Revolution.

Unlike similar vessels during their early heyday in England (when huge, untaxed fortunes could be made and spent on extravagant estates and yachts), XEBEC spent her final years enjoying the hands-on, frugal care of her last owners. They valued this yacht as their only home, certainly not as a luxury.

Hawaita

In 1932, King George V of England presented the 62-foot schooner yacht VERA MARE ("Truth Of the Sea" in Latin) to Sir Philip Hunloke, his sailing master aboard the royal yacht BRITANNIA. Among many other refinements, the schooner had stainless steel rigging, a very rare feature at the time of her launch, but the yacht was also a masterpiece of naval architecture, designed by J. & M. Soper and built by Berthon Boat Company at Lymington, Hants, England.

Well, even royals and nobles must leave behind their possessions behind when departing this cruel world, but this sad requirement gives ordinary folk an opportunity to inherit and enjoy those very same possessions. Almost 50 years after VERA MARE first felt the ocean under her, this schooner had become instead the live-aboard haven of a young English couple, charter skipper David Power and his wife Jennifer, along with their baby daughter. During the intervening years, the yacht had been renamed HAWAITA and had traveled throughout southern France and the Mediterranean. The Powers had made Spain's beautiful Costa del Sol their adopted home port.

When HAWAITA has served as a charter yacht, she benefits from the sliding wooden partition between the spacious main cabin and the skipper's cozy aft cabin — which has its own separate hatch and companionway steps, allowing direct access to the cockpit. Deep Oriental rugs silence the floorboards, and in summer a removable canvas awning protects against the hot Spanish sun.

Surprisingly, the Powers have had to "update" almost nothing inside their little royal schooner. HAWAITA's interior would be recognizable by her original owners and guests, who probably would use and appreciate the few modern conveniences hidden aboard the old schooner.

Fair Sarae

This 103-foot English staysail schooner suffered briefly with the names WHITE BITCH and EROS II (it's a long story), but her present owner, Lucy Bancroft of San Francisco, California, chose "Sarae" — a name used for generations in her mother's family. Built in 1937 by Brooke Motor Craft Company, Lowestoft, England, and designed by William McC. Meek & Sidney Graham, this yacht is heavily built to survive even mid-winter Atlantic storms. The design was based on the schooner-yacht MABEL TAYLOR, built in 1931 at Shelbourne, Nova Scotia, for the Grand Banks fishery. Solid Burma teak plank on steel frames and deck beams make this schooner incredibly tough and possibly iceberg-proof. (Only a Titanic fool would doom his vessel by uttering the forbidden adjective "unsinkable").

Much of FAIR SARAE's rich interior paneling was made with seasoned elm salvaged from London's old Waterloo Bridge. Even in such a large yacht, careful attention was paid to maximizing storage space and easy access to all compartments. Also, most of her original interior was her owners' exclusive domain, with only the forward third of the yacht used for crew quarters, the galley, a well-stocked pantry, and a huge refrigerator suitable for freezing whole sheep.

FAIR SARAE was, for many years, available for charter in the Caribbean islands, and hopefully she will remain available occasionally to the general public. Her classic style is certainly a special treat for anyone who has been subjected to the tacky interiors of sardine-can hotel suites. And there's nothing like all that varnished and natural teak surrounding you, perhaps in the cockpit when you sip your morning coffee.

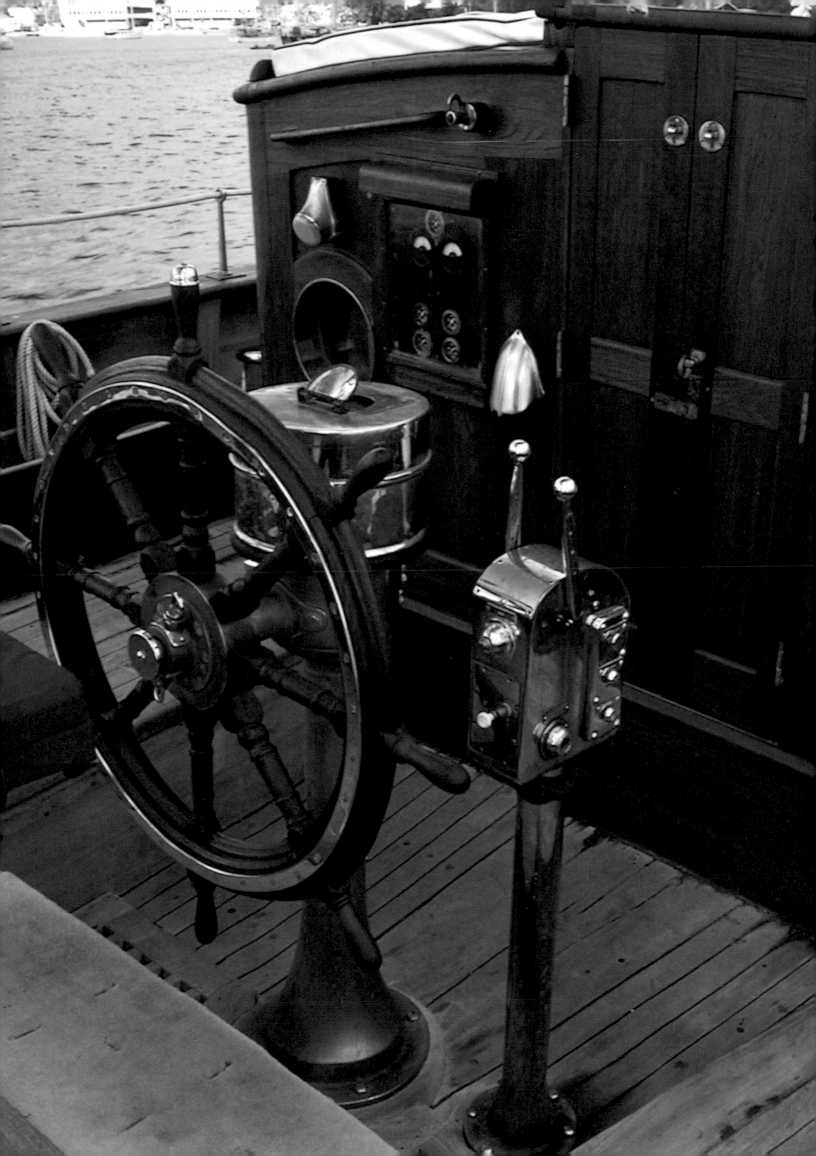

Lindø

In 1976, the Baltic trader LINDØ represented Denmark in the *Operation Sail Tall Ships* appearance and the United States' Bicentennial celebration in New York Harbor. Despite her massive construction and a hull form which only a cargo agent could love, this 92-foot, three-masted topsail schooner won an overall third place in Operation Sail's Transatlantic Races. Upon arrival in New York, LINDØ was visited and much admired by two American veterinarians, who promptly bought the schooner (under the auspices of the newly-formed Atlantic Schooner Association) and sent her to the Caribbean to begin charter work.

Passengers aboard this and other large, traditional wood sailing vessels get to enjoy as many scenic attractions and exotic refreshments as they might find with a hotel and restaurant ashore, but LINDØ also offers literally an "inside look" at our shared maritime history. Between her launch in 1928 (as the two-masted schooner LINDØ in Pukavik, Sweden) and her last cargo run in 1969, this hardworking vessel made 43 crossings of the Atlantic Ocean, carrying lumber, salted fish, grain, and nearly everything else in the way of bulk freight. She visited Nova Scotia, Central America, Iceland, and Spain; and even before her reconstruction in 1970, she could easily have kept on hauling cargo.

Much of the massive oak structure inside LINDØ was left exposed and a major part of the finished interior, reminding all who visit that they are aboard what is, in fact, a small ship, strong enough to carry tons of heavy cargo through the oceans' worst weather. Most new sailors, during their first few nights afloat sleep rather well anyway, but sleeping aboard LINDØ is very secure indeed.

Preparing meals for a large sailing vessel's captain, crew, and paying passengers is serious business, demanding an experienced, professional cook, as well as some well-trained assistants (assuming that the crew and passengers aren't counted among the galley slaves). It's even more of an accomplishment when one considers that all that food preparation happens in a confined space which often rocks back and forth, always threatening to slide the utensils, cutlery, pots and pans, and human occupants into one heap on the floor. If you are accustomed to grateful prayer immediately before consuming your dinner, be doubly grateful when your ship's cook can deliver a six-course meal aboard a 250-ton sailing vessel on the high seas. Pray that you don't lose that cook, in other words.

insulation is a must, along with a vertical, top-loading freezer designed to prevent cold air inside from simply flowing out every time the freezer is opened.

A well-equipped galley is a welcome luxury, but LINDØ depends much more on the equipment and sail-handling gear on deck — especially on the aft deck, where only a small ship's wheel and brass compass binnacle control the schooner's course. Extending aft and supporting the ship's rowboat are a pair of heavy, wooden davits. A companion-way leads down from the helm directly into the aft cabin, so that the captain can scurry back on deck in emergencies, without first having to go forward. This narrow deck area is where the captain gives the schooner's course, takes precise celestial observations, and confronts a following sea during storms.

Dry and refrigerated storage in any seagoing vessel requires a lot of planning. High humidity is the obvious main concern, but experienced ship's cooks have learned the virtues and disadvantages of different containers made of various materials. (For example, glass jars can be easily sterilized and sealed but break too easily.) Refrigeration uses a phenomenal amount of energy/fuel, so highly efficient

Condor

The design of "high-performance" racing sailboats is as much a matter of fashion as common sense. One year, the sailing crowd likes no-compromise, damn-the-torpedoes extreme racers, and a few years later the popular choice is a speedy yet family-friendly sailing yacht with "resale value." Many new yacht owners get caught in this cycle, and a few yacht designers do very well year after year, feeding the frenzy for "something faster than the other guys have."

Now and then, the international yachting community settles on a racing-measurement system that forcefully requires seaworthiness and family-style accommodations (instead of ultralight bunks which only a hardened deck gorilla could love). This means that sailing yachts designed to such a rule must be well-built, stable, and able to carry their crews in safety and comfort. What a concept!

The 50-foot sloop CONDOR was built back in 1954, when racing sailboats were a bit conservative, heavier, and intended for habitation by actual humans. Designed with a yawl rig by K. Aage Neilson, and built by Cantieri Baglietto, Varazze, Italy, the yacht was originally named TIOGA and raced under the ownership of Bradley P. Noyes of Marblehead, Massachusetts. Her performance in the 1955 Havana Race was praised in *Yachting Magazine*, and the yawl became a frequent winner in races sponsored by the New York Yacht Club. That's the good news.

The bad news is that, like many other well-traveled racing yachts, CONDOR once sank during a hurricane (when it was still christened TIOGA), but was very fortunate to get salvaged and completely repaired by Maine boatbuilder Paul Luke. The dunking and brief submersion didn't do serious damage to the traditional teak deck planking, but much of the interior needed refinishing or replacement.

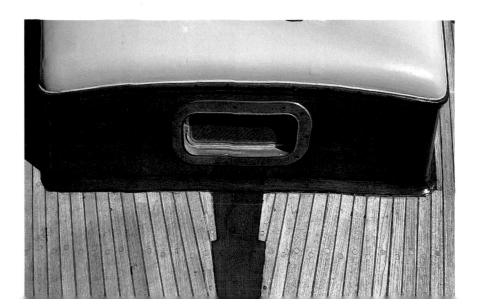

ONDOR's interior of sky-blue enamel and natural peruba wood is a major credit to Paul Luke's skill at yacht restoration and cabinetmaking. But much of the interior and deck gear, and certainly the sloop's powerful sailplan, are the recent accomplishments of Franz Schattauer, a master sailmaker in Seattle, Washington. Schattauer and his family dedicated much effort to documenting CONDOR's early racing years and succession of East Coast own-

ers (including the nonprofit Maine Maritime Academy), and the sloop also shows how a yachting-industry professional sets up and maintains his own boat. Hint: Fix it right the first time and you won't have to spend time and money on it again later.

The aft cabin in this yacht is a perfect example of soft, warm, natural wood being allowed, by itself, to "decorate" an interior. Very little color was added with paint or fabrics, and the effort put into maintenance has been

mostly a matter of careful varnish and routine vacuum-cleaning. CONDOR is very much a "family yacht," with all the important changes and projects discussed in advance by all interested parties.

CONDOR has a mix of old and new, not only in her simplified sloop rig, but in the selective use of modern sail-handling equipment, steering gear, and safety equipment. Despite the changes, one important aspect of the yacht's interior and deck design has been preserved: Nothing has been added unless it significantly improves sailing qualities, safety, or comfort below deck. CONDOR's uncluttered deck and powerful rig are intended to take Schattauer's family and guests quickly and comfortably anywhere they want to go. It's merely an added attraction that the yacht can sign up for the occasional weekend race and win it easily — not bad for a yacht which once nearly disappeared in a Caribbean hurricane!

Zorra

One of the most frequent questions from new (and sometimes even experienced) sailors is "Why is one sailing rig better than another?" The implied question that lurks underneath is "Which sailboat should I buy?" Let me give both a complicated answer and and a very simple one. The complicated explanation is partly obvious: Sailboats operate in a very wide variety of weather conditions, with crews of widely varying skill and number, and so on. Also, historic considerations come into play if a sailing yacht is in any way intended as a "replica" of some traditional sailing vessel, especially a working craft.

Less obvious is that divided rigs (with more than one mast) and older sail shapes (gaff rig, square, lug, etc.), along with more elaborate sail-handling gear, were necessities back when sail fabrics were made with much weaker and heavier organic fibers, and those cotton or flax sails had to be supported by correspondingly more elastic, heavier ropes and wooden spars. A divided sailplan may be absolutely essential if the captain's goal is simply to arrive alive somewhere across the sea, but his ship has a fragile set of sails, a heavy and too-flexible rig, and a small crew. Today's "high-aspect-ratio" sloop rigs, with a single mainsail and single foresail (and sometimes a spinnaker), are the result of vastly improved, stronger sail fabrics, lightweight aluminum masts, and very strong metal-wire stays to support the single tall mast.

The simple answer would be "Buy whatever sailboat you can safely handle and afford." This assumes that the owner and crew have already mastered the size of boat and the type of rig being considered for purchase (a wise approach). But I'd like to strongly suggest that modern sailors pause now and then and think about the advantages, despite added complexity and expense, of older, divided rigs. First, you can, generally speaking, set a greater sail area on a yacht that has a bowsprit and more than one mast; that sail area may be spread much lower, which reduces aerodynamic efficiency, but this trait also keeps the yacht from heeling quite as much. Again, a smaller, less muscular, crew can handle a divided sailplan more easily. Finally, a divided sailplan is easy to balance, and even permits self-steering in some cases.

So those are some arguments in favor of an extra mast or two. Equally persuasive may be a photo of the 73-foot yawl ZORRA at anchor in the Caribbean. Unlike most other sailboat rigs, which tend to "hunt" around their mooring, a yawl can leave its diminutive "jigger," or mizzensail, set while furling the jib and mainsail, and the yawl will ride straight and steady in nearly any breeze. Just right for a calm breakfast or cocktail hour.

Cutting holes in the top or bottom of a boat hull goes against common sense and every instinct that experienced yacht designers bring to their delicate work. Nevertheless, human crew and passengers demand some amount of natural light, which prevents claustrophobia below deck and anyway is significantly cheaper to provide than is electric illumination. Making a waterproof opening for a deck prism or translucent hatch is easy work for a capable boatbuilder, but keeping that opening leakproof over many years can be tricky.

ZORRA's designers took a gamble when they specified a deck prism directly over a cabin bunk, but the only damage appears to have been some slight water seepage and staining of interior wood. On a busy charter yacht such as this, it's bad

public relations to moisten a sleeping guest with unexpected deck leaks.

ZORRA ("Foxy Lady") was designed by Illingworth & Primrose, Emsworth, England, and built in 1965 by Cantiere Navaltecnica, Anzio, Italy. The yacht immediately went to work collecting silver trophies while racing in the Mediterranean, but her original handicap-rating, in accordance with the Royal Offshore Racing Club, was suddenly made irrelevant by acceptance worldwide of the new International Offshore Racing Rule (which has since then been rudely trampled as well). So this yawl went from being state-of-the-art to "obsolete" in a matter of months — assuming that one should take seriously the ever-volatile, crazy business of racing-sailboat measurement. ZORRA is still just as fast as she ever was, and she has lasted longer than most handicap-rating systems ever do.

Dulcidry

Selling yacht paint and varnish is hard work. It's all just expensive, toxic juice, but customers expect their bottom paint to make up for errors in steering and sail-handling, helping their yacht to forge ahead and win races, or at least to fend off barnacles and seaweed for the next century or two. Likewise, new varnish often gets applied over greasy, old varnish, or wet wood, or several layers of pristine dust and sand, with the painter's confident expectation that their miracle varnish will somehow make that inadequately prepared yacht interior outshine all others.

So the smart paint manufacturer (and that's what Italy's Veneziani Paint Company surely is) will scout about and offer some promising yacht designer or builder a chance to receive free paint in exchange for "promotional consideration." Everyone benefits, and the paint company gets its product visible out in front of the public. The 36-foot, "3/4-Ton Racer" DULCIDRY (designed by Luca Taddei) was given some space-age Veneziani polyurethane varnish for her glitzy wooden hull, which makes perfect sense, except when this hot racer zooms out ahead of other competitors and is nearly lost from sight.

I caught up with DULCIDRY in the postcard-beautiful seaside port of Lerici, where owner Giorgio Musso lives and frequently races his sleek yacht. In any context other than competitive racing, his yacht's laminated okume/cedar/spruce hull might be considered "just for pretty." But aircraft and racing-sailboat designers will recognize a structural system that uses longitudinal wood stiffeners very intelligently, producing a very strong hull for that highly stressed sailplan. Other details which might be subtle are an unusually wide forward hatch to allow fast sail changes, and an upwardly-aimed spotlight hidden below a transparent, waterproof window in the foredeck.

Allow me one final comment about those spruce "longitudinals" which stiffen the hull's dark inner surface. These highly-efficient structural members have one disadvantage when compared with traditional transverse frames (oriented vertically and perpendicular to a boat's length). When moisture collects and slides down along a hull interior with longitudinals, hopefully that water will find some method of drainage down along the longitudinals' lowest points. Even then, keeping the upper edges of longitudinals (or any other horizontal surface in a yacht) dry can be a nuisance. It helps if the hull interior can withstand the occasional spray from a garden hose.

Nearly every wooden interior component you see in these pictures is either a fundamental part of DULCIDRY's lightweight hull or at least is securely bonded to it and adds its strength to the whole assembly. Even the engine box, companionway steps, galley counter, and navigator's table contribute to the system of rigid compartments which keep this racing hull from distorting under the combined stress of sea and sails. Only the gimballed stove, stainless steel sink, and icebox could be considered deadweight (until lunchtime, that is).

Worth mention also is that modern, laminated-wood hulls almost always include a lot of marine-grade plywood, a fantastic material that earlier generations of boatbuilders could only dream about. In DULCIDRY, that plywood is used for structural bulkheads, as floorboards, and also for very simple, easily-built compartments for stowing dinner plates and bowls. (See those T-shaped slots in the plywood panel behind the white-laminate galley counter?)

Sfizio and Stradivari

I've always admired racing sailboats which show a purely artistic abandon, and Neapolitan yacht-designer Mino Simeone certainly seems to enjoy wild colors and unconventional deck design. But don't let appearances fool you. Simeone's 25-foot racing sloop SFIZIO, designed to the International Offshore Rule "1/4-Ton" rating (the term has nothing to do with the boat's actual weight), may assault the senses with its zigzag red/green/white paint job, but this is a hardcore racing machine. SFIZIO's deck and cockpit, which look like some sort of high-tech collage artwork, are bristling with winches and ropes which all serve very important purposes when tuning a sailplan for international competition.

Within SFIZIO's cockpit, the floor is just as colorful as the hull and deck above, but close-up inspection reveals that sand has been mixed into the paint to produce a very effective, easily repaired "nonskid" surface (which is also good for generating nasty scrapes on exposed elbows and knees). Nearly all of the boat's running rigging and sails can be adjusted by the crew while never leaving the cockpit. (They'll have plenty to do up on deck when it's time to raise or douse the big spinnaker.)

A quick comment might be appropriate here about the "transom" — on the stern of most sailboats, that flat or curved panel on which the yacht's name is normally painted, and which also bears more significant items such as electric stern lights, rescue equipment, possibly a dinghy (aboard larger vessels), and so on. Much hot air is expended by sailing folk intent on proving that either traditional or modern "reverse" transoms (raked at a forward angle as in SFIZIO) are superior, or at least safer, with the whole discussion getting quite weird when one tries to get to the bottom of phrases such as canoe stern, double-ender, counter stern, cruiser stern, spoon stern, and (my favorite) the always-exotic "fantail." The neophyte should be cautioned that yachting folks often become illogically partisan about just one style of sailboat. Don't forget that the rear end of a yacht should derive its form from the vessel's specific intended function, just like anything else. If you're intrigued by this sort of naval architecture, I would ask for advice from some level-headed yacht designer who has imagined and drawn a great variety of "buttocks" and "overhangs" during his or her career. Someone with a sense of humor.

SFIZIO provides a tremendous number of deck-design ideas for both racing and cruising sailboats. First is that wrap-around, semicircular track and its "traveler" which allows the mainsheet block to connect to the optimum point under the swinging boom, so that the mainsail can be trimmed and tensioned perfectly. Note that the outer ends of the traveler tracks are raised up slightly with long, tapered wooden wedges bonded to the dome-shaped deck; this keeps the boom at a constant angle to the mast, and the mainsail under constant tension, as the traveler assembly moves across the deck.

Opaque white paint or fiberglass "gelcoat" is the best bet for decks which must survive hot sunlight, but that isn't the only option. In mild climates, or if an owner can keep a boat under cover when not in use, the deck treatment can get more creative (assuming that the deck still doesn't leak and remains structurally sound). Aboard SFIZIO, the cedar strips from which the deck was laminated are completely visible through a nonskid coating of clear epoxy and tiny, transparent glass balls, applied over a clear fiberglass/ epoxy sheath. Assuming that you don't normally drop bowling balls on this deck, it will serve just fine for this little yacht.

The sliding plywood hatch aboard SFIZIO is designed to be just strong enough to support a bouncing crewmember. As spray lands on the hatch and flows to either side, the dripping water falls into a hidden gutter and safely

runs aft into the cockpit. Twin compasses allow the crew-member at the helm to check SFIZIO's course easily, even when the entire crew is "hiked out" on either side to compensate for the sailboat's normal angle of heel.

There isn't much to say about SFIZIO's spartan interior, except that this is, of course, a competition-only

"daysailer" with an absolute minimum of weight aboard. An interesting point about this yacht's all-wood construction is that the laminated ash-and-elm frames, in some cases, form a continuous loop inside the hull's cross-section. It looks pretty cool, but its real purpose is to help prevent any weak joints in the lightweight frames.

STRADIVARI is a 34-foot sloop designed by Mino Simeone to the International Offshore Rule "3/4-Ton" rating. Her musician owner, Antonio Fiorentino, wanted a very fast cruiser/racer with far more equipment and "accommodations" than are found aboard the stripped-out SFIZIO. STRADIVARI, by most people's standards, offers a fairly no-frills environment, festooned with coiled ropes, electronics, and sail gear, but at least there's a comfortable shower, toilet, galley and stove, and decent bunk cushions. Not luxurious, of course, just comfortable.

On deck, STRADIVARI shows how a different owner may require a totally different "look" aboard what is still a serious racer. I especially like the simulated teak planking; it's real teak, all right, but it's actually thin strips of this dense, heavy, expensive wood, glued down on a laminate of mahogany plywood and okume. Another nice touch is the laminated wood tiller-extension, which allows the helmsman to misbehave as if he were aboard a little racing dinghy — by crawling up and joining the rest of the crew high on the windward rail.

Like the smaller SFIZIO, STRADIVARI has a laminated wood hull and interior with almost nothing added to the exposed structure (except waterproof epoxy and varnish). Storage cabinets in the forepeak are simply plywood boxes, securely bonded along their entire edges to the surrounding hull and deck. Bunks have hinged plywood lids to allow heavy gear, clothes, and equipment to be stowed as low as possible in the boat, so that hull stability is either unaffected or actually improved.

The laminated deck frames, plywood bulkheads, and deck laminate in STRADIVARI are straightforward as far as yacht construction goes (it's the original design that's rocket science!) This hull and deck could easily be built in one's backyard with a minimum of power tools, assuming that one had access nearby to a lumber mill willing to cut a few small loads of specially-dimensioned strips or veneers. This special milling is routine and can be fairly cheap if you shop for prices well in advance. You can even ask a yacht designer to stick to woodstrip sizes which are already commonly available. If building with these techniques is something you'd like to undertake, here's a simple plan:

First, find out what the most authoritative books are on the subjects of wood/ epoxy construction, hull laminating systems, and traditional wood boatbuilding. (Many of the same assembly concepts apply to both plank-on-frame and laminated hulls.) Memorize these books. Subscribe to a few boatbuilding magazines while you're at it; they are both encourag-

ing and filled with helpful horror stories about amateur boatbuilding being the Number One cause of failed marriages and so on.

Second, practice by building a laminated wood baby cradle, or a waterproof, varnished-cedar camper shell for your truck, or an all-out, multi-compartmented "entertainment center" to hold all your stereo and TV toys. The worst that can happen is that you don't mix the glue correctly, or you leave big air pockets between wood layers, or all your wood was too wet, and

so you end up burning the whole affair in the fireplace. Do this instead of messing up your first boatbuilding project (very demoralizing and expensive).

Third, buy in advance and store all the wood, glue, fasteners, tools, and paper towels you will need for your project. It's amazing how many excellent owner-built boats get exactly halfway through their construction process before their starry-eyed builders sit down and calculate that they won't have enough money to finish their project during the foreseeable future.

Selkie

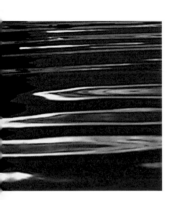

While on the subject of successful, owner-built, small yachts, let us consider the Friendship Sloop SELKIE ("Mermaid" in ancient Irish). Boatbuilder Jim Lyons grew up with virtually no exposure to sailing, and his decision to build this classic little sailboat, modeled after the traditional fishing craft of Friendship, Maine, came only after taking a marine-carpentry course at Seattle Community College. He also read the late Howard Chapelle's book *American Small Sailing Craft*. (Chapelle's many superb books could be blamed for having seduced perhaps a third of all amateur boatbuilders in America into their sinful ways.)

Using Chapelle's plans for the Maine fishing sloop PEMAQUID (from the National Museum of History and Technology, Smithsonian Institution), Lyons built SELKIE as both his personal yacht and as a convincing demonstration of his woodworking skills — which had developed when he did repair work on Alaskan fishing vessels.

SELKIE is only 25 feet long on deck, so interior components serve multiple functions whenever possible. The best example of this is a portable chest which serves as a maneuverable dining-table, while also containing silverware storage and a gimbaled alcohol stove. Bunk tops, of course, are hinged to allow storage of clothes and gear underneath.

Friendship Sloops come in many sizes and with a few important variations. The basic form, however, serves a basic purpose which modern yachts might do well to imitate: carrying a small crew safely and comfortably through good or bad weather, all the while transporting a precious cargo as quickly as possible. Even if you aren't catching and selling lobsters, your sailboat should always take good care of you (and your favorite cargo) — not the other way around.

Sea Cloud

If you dabble in the stock market, then the name "E.F. Hutton" should ring a loud bell for you. Edward F. Hutton, the man who founded a powerful stockbrokerage firm, seems to have had a major interest also in large, black sailing yachts, for he owned a series of five of them, all named HUSSAR. The fifth — the future SEA CLOUD — would be the largest privately-owned sailing yacht ever built. Hutton actually gave this four-masted barque, complete with captain and uniformed crew, to his bride, Marjorie Merriweather Post, as a wedding gift. Miss Post (a breakfast cereal heiress) got a divorce after a few years as Mrs. Hutton but kept her yacht, which she had painted white and renamed SEA CLOUD.

The fact that America's upper crust was playing with this kind of money, in an era when many American children were starving and their parents were unemployed, does rather diminish the luster of this yacht, so I try to view it today as a public museum piece. Filled with some of the most expert woodworking and the most creative interior design imaginable, SEA CLOUD was rescued in recent years by a German consortium and made available for international charter (so for the price of a very nice hotel vacation, you could instead relax aboard this unique, floating palace). SEA CLOUD had been kicked around in the Caribbean and Panama, had even done some submarine-chasing during World War II, and was destined either for the steel-scrap mills or for yet another few years with some low-budget island dictator.

When an interior designer has an immense yacht to furnish, and a virtually unlimited budget to work with, then there's room for a little fun. SEA CLOUD contains woodworking, paintings, rugs, light fixtures, and even bathrooms which would look right at home in the finest estate mansions and five-star hotels. The barque today offers a wide range of charter accommodations; the most expensive cabins and suites, along with the shared public rooms, are magnificent showcases for the work of master carvers, marble artisans, and painters who are now forgotten.

Some specifications would indicate just how grandiose is this unique sailing ship: length, overall/sparred, 353 feet; length on deck, 315 feet; and displacement, 7,780,120 pounds. SEA CLOUD's total sail area is 32,280 square feet without the main skysail.

Designed by Stevens & Cox, New York, and built in 1931 by the Krupp/Germania Shipyard, Kiel, Germany, this riveted-steel barque has four 1,500-horsepower Enterprise diesel engines.

Allow me a final note here, concerning the use of marble and gold aboard private yachts. Marble, of course, is very dense and heavy, and it isn't quite as saltwater-proof as one might imagine; think twice if a yacht designer mentions its possible use in your 40-foot sailboat. Gold, however, should be used wherever possible in yacht interiors. It doesn't tarnish (ever), comes in a nice range of colorful alloys, is as malleable in its pure form as any decorative metal needs to be, and certainly helps a yacht maintain its resale value. The high density of gold is not a problem if this metal is used in moderation.

Zivio!

The yawl ZIVIO! gets its name from a Yugoslav greeting which translates roughly as "all the love you can endure." Designed by Robert Henry and David Cluett, the yacht was built in 1963 by DeDood & Sohn, Bremen, Germany. Fast and very fancy at the same time, ZIVIO! combines traditional wooden construction, an extremely detailed Old World interior, and modern performance. She was unusual at the time of her launch because of her raised, central cockpit, separating the aft owner's cabin and the main cabin, and because of the "reverse" transom panel facing upwards at her stern. To this list of special attributes, one should add that beautiful, varnished exterior and gold leaf lettering.

Specifications and construction details: length, overall, 42 feet; beam, maximum, 11 feet, 10 inches; displacement, 25,525 pounds; and double-planked African mahogany on white oak

frames, bronze-fastened. ZIVIO! shows some of the best deck construction possible, especially in her teak deck planks and traditional "canvassed cabin top." (Canvas is glued and painted in place over a wooden deckhouse roof.) Below deck, some of the choicest mahogany I've ever seen was used lavishly, yet with incredibly precise joinery and decorative paneling.

One hull-construction detail in ZIVIO! might escape your attention, so let me get back to that "double-planked" business. Double planking is a labor-intensive, time-consuming process which, logically enough, almost doubles the time required to plank a hull. Double planking also produces a wooden hull which frequently doesn't leak! Between the two layers of wood plank a cloth barrier is sometimes applied, and then saturated with toxic paint or even varnish, which almost guarantees that water will not penetrate.

The main cabin layout in ZIVIO! is not very different from many new fiberglass cruisers. The galley has been located very close to the main companionway steps, so that prepared meals or drinks can be handed up directly on deck or into the cockpit. The navigator's station is also close to the companionway, so that course changes can be discussed quickly with the helm.

The deckhouse construction, viewed from down below in ZIVIO!, is both a lesson in artistic design and a textbook example of meticulous structural woodworking. On deck, a sliding hatch and the canvased cabin roof are elegant, while also protecting the yacht's crew from rain and spray; tiny metal snaps are used to attach protective canvas panels when the yacht spends extensive time in the marina. A portable backrest makes leaning against the hard cockpit a comfortable experience for passengers.

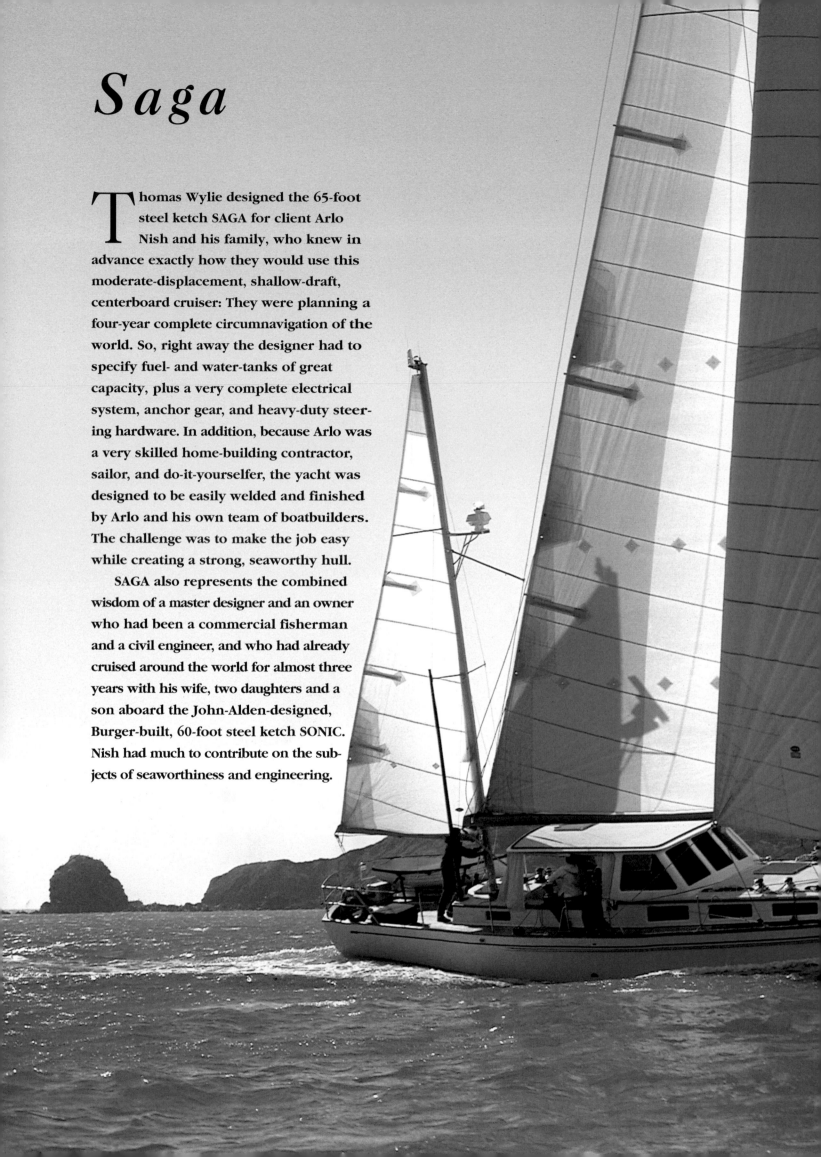

Saga

Thomas Wylie designed the 65-foot steel ketch SAGA for client Arlo Nish and his family, who knew in advance exactly how they would use this moderate-displacement, shallow-draft, centerboard cruiser: They were planning a four-year complete circumnavigation of the world. So, right away the designer had to specify fuel- and water-tanks of great capacity, plus a very complete electrical system, anchor gear, and heavy-duty steering hardware. In addition, because Arlo was a very skilled home-building contractor, sailor, and do-it-yourselfer, the yacht was designed to be easily welded and finished by Arlo and his own team of boatbuilders. The challenge was to make the job easy while creating a strong, seaworthy hull.

SAGA also represents the combined wisdom of a master designer and an owner who had been a commercial fisherman and a civil engineer, and who had already cruised around the world for almost three years with his wife, two daughters and a son aboard the John-Alden-designed, Burger-built, 60-foot steel ketch SONIC. Nish had much to contribute on the subjects of seaworthiness and engineering.

His decision to build a steel hull came from that material's many advantages, including consistent, high strength, tremendous resistance to puncture, and ease of repair. (Any skilled welder around the world can cheaply fix a dent in SAGA's hull in a matter of hours.)

This big boat has some unusual proportions, including a ketch rig with so small a mizzen that it might qualify the yacht as a yawl or modern cutter. Draft is 6 feet, 6 inches, or 14 feet, 9 inches with the centerboard down. Maximum beam is a generous 17 feet, 10 inches, and displacement 68,000 pounds (of which 13,000 pounds is lead and steel ballast). Sail area, without the little mizzen, is 1,861 square feet.

SAGA has a roomy pilothouse with a permanent roof, and there's bench seating for family and guests around the helm. Unbreakable-plastic windows forward are arranged to allow 360-degree visibility. In bad weather, removable canvas panels can be unrolled and lowered to seal the pilothouse sides and aft archway entirely. The wide deck and cabin tops are unusually free of unnecessary obstacles.

But SAGA's interior really sets this yacht apart from the crowd. Her owners had very detailed plans for cabin proportions, lighting, plenty of seating, storage areas, and especially the well-equipped galley — which boasts a large convection oven, an equally large microwave oven, double sinks, various smaller electric appliances, and a durable, wrap-around CORIAN® countertop (an investment in cash and weight which not all boats can

afford). Freezer and refrigerator storage compartments are very large, which means that SAGA's electric generator and battery systems are necessarily oversize. From all this, you can probably tell that the yacht's owner and family expected to host a considerable number of parties and elaborate dinners aboard.

Before SAGA departed for her 'round-the-world cruise, I was made privy to a design secret which seems useful whenever a yacht expects to be boarded and taxed for bottles of liquor brought into foreign countries. SAGA's water tanks are connected and cleverly subdivided so that a water-supply line leading to the wet bar sink in the saloon/entertainment area can (with a quick turn of a well-hidden handle) instead supply a steady stream of "distilled spirits" — which, not being bottled or easily discovered, will not be taxed.

Whitehawk

The 92-foot wooden ketch WHITEHAWK is that rare combination of very modern technology and materials, very traditional appearance, and thoroughly high-performance naval architecture — a combination for which designer Bruce P. King has become deservedly famous. This laminated wood/epoxy yacht was commissioned by Californian Phil Long and built in 1978 by O. Lie-Nielson (Lee's Boat Shop, Rockland, Maine). Her interior is as flawlessly executed as anything found aboard yachts built a century ago.

One of the places where a "classic" yacht is expected to demonstrate her builder's creativity and artistic flair is on the nameboard and stern decorations. I was lucky to see WHITE-HAWK's immense hull out of the water, once during the final stages of her construction, and once again during minor maintenance before her first long voyage to the Caribbean. The first time was a good chance to study the hidden construction details, but the second photo opportunity allowed me to stand directly below that lovely carved nameboard, carved white hawk with wings outstretched, and carved ropework around the transom.

WHITEHAWK displaces 165,000 pounds, has a maximum beam of 20 feet, 6 inches, and uses a very large ballasted "daggerboard" hydraulically lowered to increase draft from 7 feet, 5 inches to 16 feet, 10 inches. Overall/sparred length is 109 feet. Construction is three diagonal layers of cedar veneer, bronze-nailed and epoxy-glued over longitudinal cedar strip plank; a final exterior layer of longitudinal mahogany veneer was attached with plugged bronze screws. The complete hull laminate is 2.5 inches thick, coated completely inside and out with epoxy. The hull has yellow pine floor timbers, laminated white oak keelson and sheer-clamp, and a teak deck over laminated cedar on oak deck beams. The interior is mahogany, teak, oak, and cedar, with spars made of spruce.

Selecting from all the various hardwoods available for interior construction is partly a matter of aesthetics; what contrasting grain, wood colors, and "figure" patterns will make the final interior pleasing to the eye? Another variable is the hardness and resistance to moisture or staining, along with the wood's ability to take glue, varnish, or paint as required. WHITEHAWK's interior shows that very traditional, practical decisions were made in wood selection. For example, dark African mahogany is durable, stable, beautiful, and

holds varnish well, so it com-prises most of the interior which encounters normal human traffic. Varnished teak is also used, sometimes where constant moisture or unusually heavy wear require a wood that has its own natural oils and resistance to scratches.

The softer cedar strip-plank on the inner hull surface was simply sanded, epoxy-sealed, sanded again, and then varnished. Note that most of the yacht's interior surface has no frames to stiffen the hull at regular intervals, the designer having instead

specified a slightly thicker hull laminate and reinforcing bulkheads or floor timbers only where the hull is highly stressed.

Interior hardware selection was made without any consideration toward impressing visitors and passengers. After all, WHITEHAWK is impressive enough, and gaudy hardware can actually cheapen the final result. Standard solid-brass drawer-latches are used to keep stowage secure when the yacht is under sail. In fact, many drawers and cabinets have no visible latches or hardware at all, the builders having care-fully hidden these metallic items behind the varnished wood panels. Finger-holes cut into cabinet doors, for example, allow one to pull a hidden latch so that the door opens easily. These finger-holes (and vent-holes) are decorative, can be customized to match a yacht's unique character, and have one distinct advantage: young, overly inquisitive children, when informed that large, equally inquisitive spiders lurk just inside those finger-holes, will hesitate all day before deciding to risk their digits, and by then it may be time to go home.

Navita

The 64-foot "motorsailer" ketch NAVITA has led a charmed life. Built in 1938 in Seattle, Washington, this yacht was a secret self-indulgence of the president of Boeing Airplane Company, who was in the middle of tense labor/management negotiations and didn't want his workers to know about his financial ability to go yachting. Luckily, Boeing workers won the right to unionize, and Boeing's president also got his ketch.

The raised "quarterdeck" aboard NAVITA offers absolutely no sanctuary for puddles of water, and all the major deck seams (taffrail, bulwarks, and so

on) are sealed with concave margin planks. All wood on the quarterdeck, excluding only the flagstaff, is teak. Note the compass mounted in the kingplank directly forward of the wheel. Although less intrusive than the traditional binnacle, this compass arrangement requires that the helmsman choose between looking over the bow or looking down at his or her feet. A compass at nearly eye level allows one both to follow the navigator's instructions and to discover his errors. During a foggy passage in 1940, this yacht ran aground and sank, but was subsequently salvaged.

NAVITA's specifications are as follows: designed by Walter D. Lynch and built at the Blanchard Boat Yard, in Seattle; displacement is 61,712 pounds; total sail area is 1,236 square feet; and the engine is an original 150-horsepower Buda-Lanova "Silver Crown" connected to a huge, variable-pitch propeller. Construction is Port Orford cedar on oak frames, Alaska cedar stringers, teak keel, bronze-fastened, with a canvassed cedar cabin-top and a teak deck on oak beams. Spars are spruce, and the entire interior is solid teak and oak.

A yacht's galley is where the designer's cruising experience and concern for domestic comforts have a chance to benefit his clients. Aboard this yacht, a series of owners and their cabinetmakers have also added their own personal touches. NAVITA now has a very complete, yet compact, galley, with a modern, stainless steel sink and very detailed, clever stowage shelves for plates, cups, and bowls. There's even a little ceramic soap dish, just like in your favorite Victorian "bed-and-breakfast" hotel. Stowage cabinets surrounding the galley countertop are painted glossy white, with small, unobtrusive, stainless steel latches and hinges. A fire-extinguisher is mounted almost exactly within arm's reach of the stove, but not above it, where flames would prevent quick access.

While you are admiring this lovely yacht interior and its elegant appointments, try to imagine this vessel as it might have looked in the Ultimate Hippie Year of 1968, when NAVITA had "fallen into the hands of Californians" and was caught in a famous smuggling incident by Canadian authorities. Those comfortable bunks and delicate shelves were packed with a contraband cargo rather more spicy than silverware.

After getting seized and put up for government auction, NAVITA was purchased by Herb Carroll, the owner of a Seattle jewelry store, whose favorite cargo aboard his soon-restored yacht was simply his children, grandchildren, and even great-grandchildren.

Raven

The late, great yacht designer and superb author L. Francis Herreshoff described the appearance of exposed, unpainted fiberglass boat interiors as (forgive me) "frozen snot." This vile phrase is completely accurate and politely ignores even worse attributes of cured GRP (glass-reinforced plastic) laminates: toxic chemicals, hazardous glass micro-fibers, strange smells, and so on. All commercial builders of fiberglass sailboats and motorboats, for both aesthetic and safety reasons, have learned to cover up or paint every square inch of fiberglass inside their vessels. (Paint helps to keep the fiberglass waterproof and easily cleaned as well.)

Some builders, such as the famous Nautor Company in Finland, have gone several steps further and build exquisite, all-wood, modern interiors within their high-quality fiberglass hulls. The buyer gets all the many advantages of fiberglass construction, plus an interior which is beautiful and adds considerably to the yacht's future resale value. Nautor is famous throughout the world for their "Swan" line of luxury racer/cruisers, many of which are popular in the crewed and bareboat charter trades.

The Nautor-built, 57-foot sloop RAVEN, designed by Sparkman & Stephens, New York, has an interior which is warm, elegant, and very practical.

Details

Sailors, yacht designers, and boat-builders often like to think of themselves as dashing, adventurous souls who do a better job of living life to the fullest than do mere "landlubbers." That's a little bit true, but once the decision to get one's feet wet is made, boating folk often fall victim to stale design clichés. One of these governs how the floorboards in a yacht should look: I would estimate that 95 percent of all the production sailboats out there contain the same teak-and-holly plywood floorboards. Motor yacht interiors tend instead to have identical, motel-style, pastel-color "shag" carpets which, by the way, are great incubators for all sorts of mysterious bacteria, potato chips, grease, and noxious aromas.

Admittedly, naval architects and boat-builders must work within the public's expectations of what a "yachty" interior should look like. So I guess it's my sincere wish that readers of this book will come away with greater expectations. Be open-minded when a yacht designer shows

you pictures of a laminated, completely waterproof "parquet" floor (in this case made of cherry, maple, and mahogany). It may cost more, or it may not. All a floor needs to do is support you, resist water and abrasion, and stay put. It might as well add to the unique character of your yacht, so be a little creative!

Woodworking is not the only area where classic yachts can add personality and practical value. Aboard the 62-foot, English gaff cutter TERN IV (designed by the famous Claud Worth as a gaff yawl in 1924), close inspection of a highly-decorative old doorknob reveals that it is more than beautiful — it's solid silver. Constant polishing by human hands keeps the raised pattern quite shiny, and if the captain ever lacks for emergency funds in a foreign port, he can always take some doorknobs to the local bank. I'd love to see the look on that bank teller's face.

Highly decorative and durable marine plywood is used in conjunction with laminated door frames and handholds. In the forepeak, longitudinal varnished wood slats (historically called "ceiling" long before the term was used in homes) are similar to inner planking used in traditional wooden sailboats; these slats create a comfortable surface for passengers and bedding, but allow air to circulate in these confined quarters.

On Deck

New sailors are often intimidated by the complex, intricate terminology of boating and sail-handling, and the problem is made worse by the fact that (gasp!) different sailors, even when not using different languages, sometimes use different names for the same item on deck. Advice: Let each of the differing experts have their way on their separate yachts. On the other hand, it's extremely important for safety and many other reasons to use a very clear, standard terminology aboard any one boat! If your captain refers to that massive iron whatsit over there as a "windlass" and you always thought it was a "wildcat," do everyone a favor and continue to say "windlass" during the entire voyage. One reason that safety is at stake is that captains rarely find arguments about nautical linguistics even mildly amusing — trust me on this subject. At the end of your voyage, go check an authoritative maritime dictionary and look up the correct definitions of windlass and wildcat. While you're at it, find out the difference between a capstan and a captain. (The former has slightly more cranial mass and generally better manners.)

Now that you're spooked about this stuff, here's an important secret. While keeping in mind the absolute need for clear, rapid crew communication when maneuvering at sea and in harbors, nevertheless experienced sailors gradually become fairly relaxed about the whole tangled subject of "nautical nomenclature." The really experienced old codgers even start to buy yachts, not according to how historically authentic or up-to-date they may be, but according to how comfy they feel when they sit on them. That's a nice attitude — it implies that you and your guests should be happy, at ease, and unpretentious while aboard or inside a boat. One famous old naval architect, while taking some potential clients for a brief demonstration sail aboard one of his designs, persisted in saying that he would now "turn left" or "turn right," instead of port and starboard. His passengers assumed that he was using layman's terminology for their sake, until he announced that someone else should take the helm while he went to the "potty."

I like Greek sailors. Their country has been practicing the art and science of sailing for literally thousands of years amid hundreds of rocky Mediterranean islands, so they no longer need to prove or boast of their maritime qualifications. Greeks were building superb ships and braving deep-water storms back when my ancestors were still running around dressed in nothing but blue paint, still fearful of that mysterious, briny liquid surrounding their homeland. Today, you can't ask for a better vacation

than a crewed charter voyage aboard a Greek sailing yacht. The vessel, the crew, the very air around you will make you relax.

Designed specifically as charter yachts, on many Greek motorsailers, such as the 75-foot DOXA, I have all the conveniences of a resort hotel, but my flexible itinerary, schedule, and crew make all the difference. If you decide you want to visit a particular obscure island and also have a special Greek seafood dish when you arrive, be prepared for the captain to simply alter course right then and there, followed

by instructions to the crew that the yacht's fishing nets should be brought on deck.

Be prepared, also, for the special Mediterranean style of boat-handling. For example, Greek yachts generally "back up" in close formation to a stone quay (where cafés and restaurants serve customers who especially like to dine while looking out at the row of yachts!) That means that Greek yachts nearly always have permanent boarding-ramps and related gear perched on their sterns, ready for lowering when the yacht ties up. The bow of most traditional wooden Greek sailboats is also generally quite broad, with heavy timbers to withstand pounding waves; in mild weather, it's a great place to catch the warm sunlight and talk back to the porpoises below. As for the crew, they may be relaxed and charming, but years of experience make them well-prepared for fickle Mediterranean weather. They rely on both their sturdy ship and any protective blessings or illumination which a friendly deity might want to share.

Steering is something that sailors take for granted — until something suddenly goes wrong. I was slowly steering toward a dock once aboard a heavy sailboat when the wheel in my hands abruptly stopped resisting my pressure. A little corroded cotter pin hidden away under the deck had chosen exactly the wrong moment to break, allowing the steering gear to swing completely out of control. I was barely able to reverse the engine in time and veer away from the dock while we conducted emergency repairs (having some long oars on deck proved helpful). That sort of trauma helps one appreciate why experienced yacht

designers always specify simple, rugged steering gear or stick to the old-fashional "tiller" system.

Sometimes both systems can work on the same vessel. The Greek 72-foot motorsailer IRENE still has its massive tiller exposed for emergency access, although the normal steering is now done with a wheel. The stern of this semitraditional vessel is built so that ropes leading to a dock or, temporarily (in emergency), to the short tiller, have several places to get tied up on deck.

Try to imagine three expert but amateur sailors steering their slender yawl across the stormy North Atlantic, using the simple wooden tiller and binnacle compass you see here. The 53-foot yawl DORADE was designed in 1930 by a young Olin Stephens and

sailed by him, his father, and his brother Rod Stephens, Jr. to victory in the next year's Transatlantic Race — an event traditionally dominated by enormous schooner yachts with paid, professional captains and crews. In case anyone attributed the Transatlantic win merely to good luck, DORADE later took two of Britain's Fastnet Races, the 1932 Bermuda Race (Class B), and the 1935 run from San Francisco to Honolulu. And the Stephens brothers' subsequent careers in America's Cup "12-Metre" design and other international yacht competition simply drove the point home. DORADE also gave her name to the now-ubiquitous "Dorade vent," a simple and effective system which this yacht popularized for separating spray from incoming air flow.

Even if it doesn't obviously affect navigation, or anchoring, or anything else aboard a yacht, "neatness" counts. It's part of the whole shipshape thing, which lets you concentrate on enjoying your voyage instead of where that damn screwdriver went to. Neatness also has a certain artistic value, as is evident in these photos of deck details aboard three very different wooden vessels: the Maine charter schooner MISTRESS; the live-aboard classic motor yacht COLLEEN; and the traditional Greek "caique perama" SELINI (named after the harvest moon goddess).

MISTRESS keeps the usual safety and navigational equipment near the companionway forward of her helm; that includes a portable compass, fire extinguisher, a life ring, and the usual engine controls and instrument dials. COLLEEN impressed me with her simple, spotless paint job; the blue-and-white deckhouse panels and canvased roof reveal an owner's love of cleanliness and order.

SELINI's blue-and-orange paint job and carefully secured sail-handling gear remind a sailor visiting the Mediterranean for the first time that bold patterns and colors, and lots of them, are an ancient part of Greek boat and ship design. In a land where the unrelenting sun bleaches and fades nearly everything in very little time, fresh, new colors are a welcome addition to homes and boats alike. Traditional Greek sailboats, after all, sometimes even have eyes painted at their bows — some say to help the vessel find its way — but I suspect the eyes allow each boat to admire its colorful neighbors.

Traditional sailing vessels have a wide variety of equipment and rigging that served quite well for hundreds of years before modern equivalents took their place. Navigation lights, those red and green lanterns on a vessel's port and starboard sides, indicated to approaching ships approximately which course a vessel was on and helped to avoid collisions. Each such lantern was mounted in a metal reflective frame, or against a wooden lightboard sometimes painted the same color as the lantern's radiated light. Aboard the schooner BRIGADOON, the common practice of also painting the vessel's name on the lightboard makes the schooner's name that much more readable at a distance.

As for rigging, the differences between traditional and modern sailing vessels are

too numerous to even sample here. One consistent theme is that, until about two hundred years ago, even easily-produced metals such as wrought iron, steel, copper, and bronze were still too expensive to be used carelessly or at all in normal working sailboats, so traditional rigging solutions still prevailed. Nearly all large sailing ships and most smaller craft used "deadeyes," round cylinders of some unusually dense hardwood (lignum vitae is still preferred). Deadeyes were drilled and installed in pairs, one deadeye attached indirectly to the ship, and the other directly to the lower end of a tarred-hemp or wire rope stay, so that smaller ropes could be threaded through holes in both deadeyes, tightened, and then secured. As the stays stretched, the deadeyes could easily be adjusted to take up the slack and support the mast.

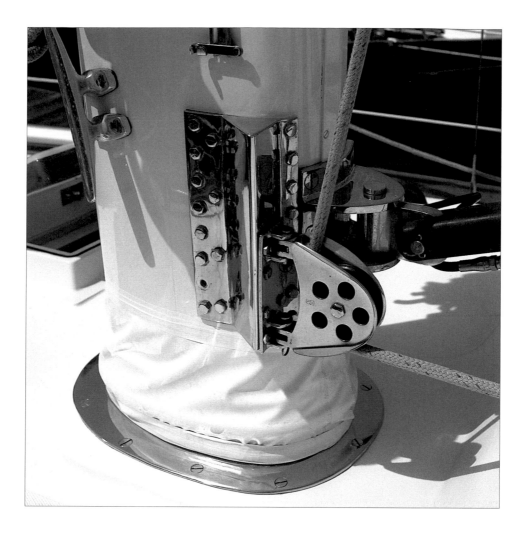

The most common practice when installing a mast on a sailboat is for the mast to pierce the deck and find support much lower from the boat's thick, rigid keel; the deck then gets a tight wooden or metal "collar" surrounding the mast to help keep it standing. The alternate approaches, to "step" the end of the mast up on deck, or to use a hinged mast connection above the deck (common in European countries, where boats frequently must pass under canal bridges), don't help to keep the mast both straight and upright under load, but these arrangements also don't create a structurally vulnerable, leaky hole in the deck.

The 92-foot topsail schooner LINDØ has a substantial wooden mast collar discreetly hidden under a snug mast "coat" of painted canvas and decorative knotwork. Its function is merely to keep water from entering the thin seam between mast and mast collar, a purpose which is served equally well aboard the Hinckley 59 ketch CLAUDIE, but with modern materials and no decoration. CLAUDIE's mast also has a hydraulic system to keep the boom above under constant tension, and there's a massive, stainless steel block attached directly to the mast.

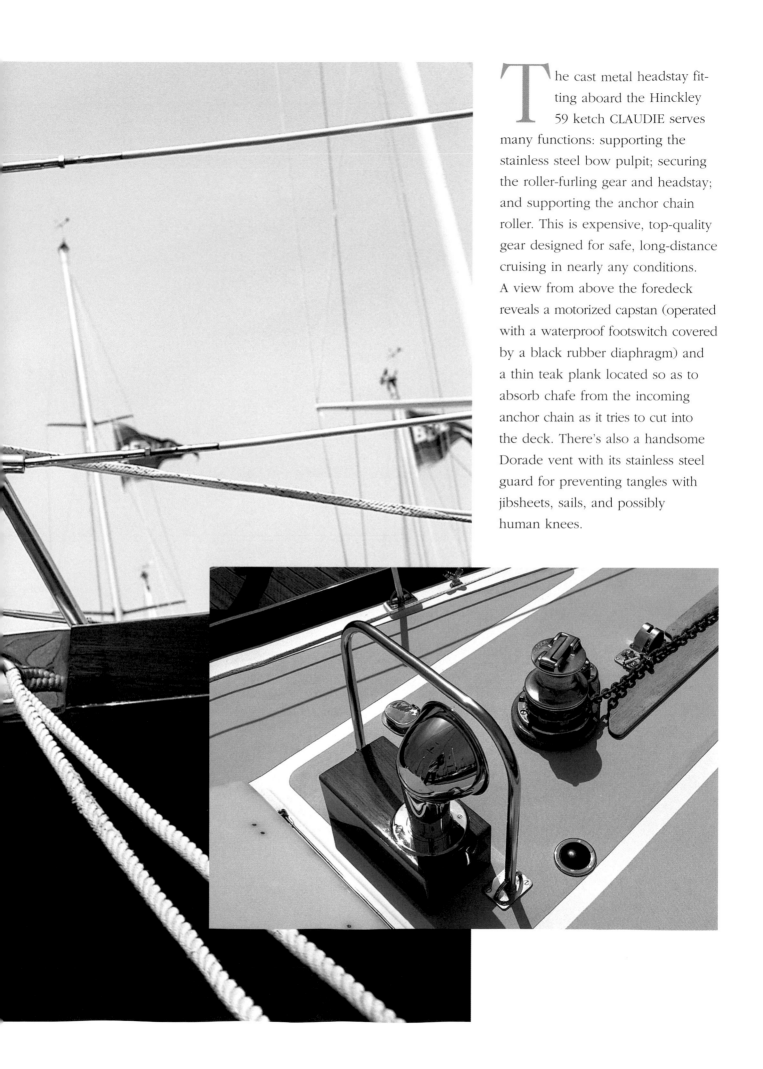

The cast metal headstay fitting aboard the Hinckley 59 ketch CLAUDIE serves many functions: supporting the stainless steel bow pulpit; securing the roller-furling gear and headstay; and supporting the anchor chain roller. This is expensive, top-quality gear designed for safe, long-distance cruising in nearly any conditions. A view from above the foredeck reveals a motorized capstan (operated with a waterproof footswitch covered by a black rubber diaphragm) and a thin teak plank located so as to absorb chafe from the incoming anchor chain as it tries to cut into the deck. There's also a handsome Dorade vent with its stainless steel guard for preventing tangles with jibsheets, sails, and possibly human knees.

The foredeck aboard the 50-foot John Alden schooner VOYAGER has two anchors stowed one above the other in chocks to port of the bowsprit bitts. Padeyes on the deck under the anchors allow them to be tied down securely with a wood cradle locking the upper anchor in place. Note also the reassuringly thick plastic top on the hatch cover; it almost compensates for the crack started in the wooden hatch itself by the hinge screws.

The traditional wooden motor yacht HERMANA carries a very substantial windlass up on her foredeck, with drums and wildcat for handling rope and chain. In contrast, the modern steel ketch SAGA has a novel below-deck arrangement which uses a single hydraulically-operated drum for hauling in and winding up a considerable length of chain. The anchor gear and its weight is kept low this way, but the entire drum with chain and anchors adds significant weight in the bow. The person operating the hydraulic gear below deck is protected from wind and waves, which normally make weighing anchor tricky on an exposed foredeck.

The 94-foot topsail schooner CALIFORNIAN has a sliding hatch with etched-glass, hinged window panels along its sides. Both the glasswork and the bronze hinges are simple enough to design and manufacture, but this vessel is noteworthy for this kind of artistic and historic detail. In addition, the hatch slides very smoothly and doesn't leak a drop!

A sliding companionway hatch aboard the 90-foot South African steel schooner ANTARES is somewhat less decorative, but reveals designer/builder Arthur C. Holgate's passion for unifying, welded-steel components to add strength while reducing weight. The forward end of the long companionway is joined to the thick, stainless steel pinrail surrounding the mast. The smoothly polished, cylindrical form of that rail allows the crew to lead halyards or other rope under it and then use it almost like a low-friction block with roller bearings. Another example of combining functions to save weight: ANTARES' foremast also serves as the galley smokestack, while the mainmast ventilates the schooner's bathrooms.

The Hinckley 59 ketch CLAUDIE has a stainless steel boarding ladder which lifts up and folds against her stern. It's a convenient, unobtrusive design so well-concealed that visitors often don't even realize the yacht has such a ladder — which is ideal for unloading a dinghy or for sending swimmers ashore when anchored near a beach.

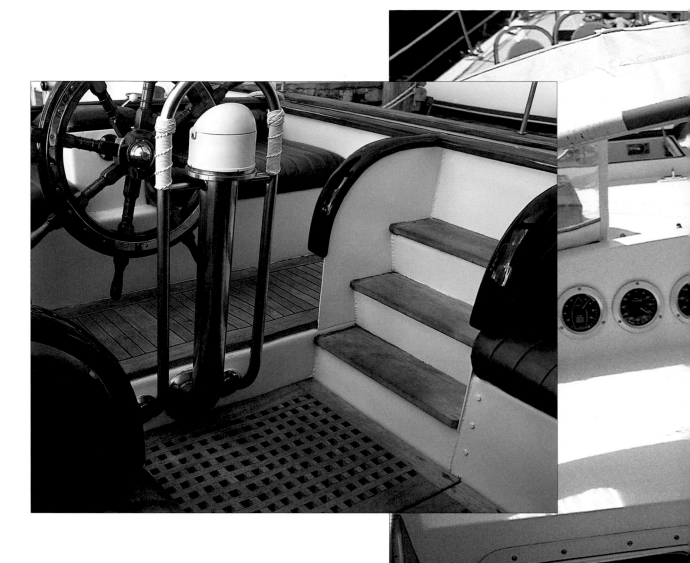

The 90-foot schooner ANTARES has a very simple, T-shaped cockpit arrangement, with steps leading up to deck level on both port and starboard. Long, upholstered benches flank both sides of the long cockpit, which has several large teak gratings underfoot; the gratings allow the cockpit to drain very quickly if ocean waves climb aboard this big, fast schooner. Just aft of the wheel and binnacle aboard ANTARES is a detachable, self-steering windvane, making this vessel possibly the largest in the world with such a device. As elegant as this cockpit appears, it is, in fact, designed to withstand heavy weather and constant attack by salt and spray, while giving the helmsman excellent visibility in all directions.

The Hinckley 59 ketch CLAUDIE has a very clean, functional deck, with a modern compass binnacle and a folding "dodger" to protect the helmsman from wind and spray. Full instrumentation in plain sight means that the helmsman is the first to know of engine problems, navigational errors, electrical anomalies, and changes in weather or boat performance.

Designed by Winthrop L. Warner and built in 1949 by Paul Luke of East Boothbay, Maine, the cutter-rigged motorsailer CONGAR is a compact, 43-foot live-aboard in which a young couple and their cat lived happily for many years. This all-wood classic has a very complete interior, with impeccable mahogany joinery and all necessary equipment, but her teak deck and sail-handling equipment is the very model of efficiency. Equipment includes self-tailing and self-storing winches, roller-furling headsail, and a self-tending staysail.

CONGAR's wide teak deck has a smooth, curved "break" right in the middle of the long superstructure. You can walk right past it or even sit on it without giving it a second thought, but then you realize that all those smooth teak planks on the cabin roof plunge down in a tight curve, much like porpoises suddenly diving in unison. Someone had to cut and plane and sand all those curved planks so that they match perfectly, and the big, chromed-bronze Dorade vent sitting right on top of the break makes the effect even more dramatic. Practical value? It's arguably stronger than a right-angle break in the deck, and could it conceivably reduce wind turbulence? Perhaps the fact that you can sit down on deck and lean comfortably against the curved break? Or maybe the designer was simply toying with a nice new "French curve" on his drafting table, and maybe he instinctively knew it would look and feel better than the usual hard-edged cabin-top.

An Invitation

A "yacht" doesn't have to be some grandiose floating palace which you can't afford. After cruising through all these photos of yacht interiors and sumptuous deck details, some readers might feel that this yachting game is simply too expensive and too difficult to comprehend. But tight finances or a lack of boating experience haven't stopped thousands of men, women, and children from getting involved in boats for the first time, whether their interest was in sailing or power- boats, modern or traditional. Some people first get their feet wet in boats when they are quite young (I was lucky to have parents who gave me an early start), but many yachting people I know were well into their child-rearing or even retirement years before they took the plunge.

Many people got started in yachting by taking a vacation at some seaside resort which offered basic sailing classes. You can even volunteer aboard some small or large boats, in exchange for sail training and a chance to pick up other maritime skills. Other people just march right into a local yacht club and ask if that club has training programs for new members with little or no boating

experience. (The answer is almost always "yes.") Some determined new boating folk carefully track down a sailing school which can lead them all the way from Beginner status through Intermediate to Advanced, followed by a test and final international certification as qualified charter-yacht skippers. (This means you can get on the phone and reserve a yacht for a few weeks just as you would a hotel room.)

Even hardcore boatbuilders can get started with little or no money. I once met a bunch of people on the waterfront in Sausalito, California who had pooled their very limited cash, tools, and boatbuilding library, and a year or two later they were sailing their own replica of Captain Joshua Slocum's famous SPRAY, in which he completed the world's first singlehanded circumnavigation. Having used only free or incredibly cheap "recycled" lumber, these SPRAY builders learned high-quality boatbuilding, teamwork, and then bluewater sailing aboard their seaworthy little ship. To them, and to anyone else who launches their dream boat against the prevailing current, this book is dedicated.